Fiston TSHIANYI WA TSHIANYI

# Handling unbalanced classes using assembly methods

Fiston TSHIANYI WA TSHIANYI

# Handling unbalanced classes using assembly methods

ScienciaScripts

**Imprint**

Any brand names and product names mentioned in this book are subject to trademark, brand or patent protection and are trademarks or registered trademarks of their respective holders. The use of brand names, product names, common names, trade names, product descriptions etc. even without a particular marking in this work is in no way to be construed to mean that such names may be regarded as unrestricted in respect of trademark and brand protection legislation and could thus be used by anyone.

Cover image: www.ingimage.com

This book is a translation from the original published under ISBN 978-620-6-70636-6.

Publisher:
Sciencia Scripts
is a trademark of
Dodo Books Indian Ocean Ltd. and OmniScriptum S.R.L publishing group

120 High Road, East Finchley, London, N2 9ED, United Kingdom
Str. Armeneasca 28/1, office 1, Chisinau MD-2012, Republic of Moldova, Europe
Printed at: see last page
ISBN: 978-620-7-86640-3

# EPIGRAPH

*"Artificial intelligence is defined as the ability of a machine to automatically learn, adapt and solve complex problems with increasing accuracy and performance that benefit society."*

**Sri Amit Ray**

# DEDICATION

To my brother, Felly MBALA TSHIANYI.

**Fiston TSHIANYI**

# ACKNOWLEDGEMENTS

First of all, we'd like to thank our only Lord and Savior, the **LORD JESUS CHRIST, for** his kindness in granting us the chance to finish our university studies.

We would also like to express our gratitude to Professor Doctor **KAFUNDA KATALAY Pierre** and **KATULUMBA NGANDU Marcel** Assistant, respectively Director and Co-Director, for having accepted to supervise this work despite their busy schedules.

We would also like to reiterate our thanks to all the professors, supervisors, assistants, lecturers and other staff at the University of Mbujimayi, Faculty of Applied Sciences, Computer Engineering Department, who, through their contributions of any kind, have guided my thinking and agreed to meet me and answer my questions during my research.

And you, my heroes, my parents, **Alidor TSHIANYI MUTOMBO** and **Mamie MOKOLA MBALA**, who have always been there for me, sacrificing everything for your children, sparing neither health nor effort. You have given me a magnificent model of hard work and perseverance, and I am indebted to you for an education of which I am proud.

Special thanks to **Deo Gracias KABULU, Felly MBALA TSHIANYI, Anita NTANGA NKASHAMA, Arlette MULEKA MBALA and**
**Freddy MFWENDE** for their unwavering support for my modest efforts.

Not to honor the contribution of our brothers, sisters, uncles, aunts, cousins and grandparents would be ingratitude; we're thinking of **Félicien MBALA KAFIONDO, Berthe MVUMBI, Naomie CIDIBI, Huguette MUADI, Merveil KABEMBA, Divine MBIAYA, Bétine MASANGU, Emmanuel MUANJI, Racheté MOKOLA.**

Finally, we would like to thank our department heads, friends and colleagues, some for their sympathy and others for their support and prayers. Our thoughts are with : **Trésor KHASA, Guy MALUMBA, Jules TSHIMPAKA, John KALALA, Marius Trésor KATENDA, Jean Luc MUTEBA, Elie NGAMBWA, Neville Ormane KAMBAJA, Nick NSANGANA, Doudou KATENDA, Emmanuel KIBUANA, Gustave KABUYA, Serge KASAMBAYI, Arnold KADIMA, Sharon MIANDABU, Bérénice LUSAMBA, Chirac KAZADI, Steven NGELEKA, Pierre Damien MUAMBA, Michael CIBANGU, Cédric MBUYI, Merveil NTUMBA, Fabrice KALUBIAKA**, etc... please find here all my gratitude.

May all those who have contributed in one way or another, far or near, but who will not see their name mentioned in the present work, may they not feel neglected, but may they find here the expression of our deep gratitude! For this and for more, we say to each and every one of you a big thank you.

**Fiston TSHIANYI**

# LIST OF ACRONYMS AND

| N° | Code / Acronym | Meaning |
|---|---|---|
| 1. | ML | Machine Learning |
| 2. | SVM | Support Vector Machine |
| 3. | IA | Artificial Intelligence |
| 4. | K-PPV | K nearest neighbors |
| 5. | KNN | K nearest neighbors |
| 6. | EM | Expectation-Maximization |
| 7. | RPG | Gradient retro propagation |
| 8. | H | Hyperplane |
| 9. | MCS | Multi classifiers systems |
| 10. | SQL | Structure query language |
| 11. | RF | Random Forest |
| 12. | RCW | Balanced Random Forest |
| **13.** | **WBF** | **Weighted Random Forest** |

# SUMMARY

This thesis deals with decision optimization using ensemblistic methods for processing unbalanced databases. To achieve this, we have used ensemblistic methods, which are based on the homogeneous combination of predictions or classifiers for better generalization.

In our final year project, we used the Credit Card Fraud Detection database to generate and evaluate the proposed model. We also chose the random forest combination method, which combines several decision trees and applies the majority voting strategy to produce an optimal prediction.

**Keywords**: Artificial intelligence, ensemblistic methods, random forest, classifier, prediction, decision tree, unbalanced classes.

# ABSTRACT

The present thesis concerns the optimization of the decision by the set methods for the treatment of unbalanced databases. To achieve this, we used set methods that are based on the homogeneous combination of predictions or classifiers for a better generalization.

In our end-of-study project, we used the Credit Card Fraud Detection database to generate and evaluate the proposed model. We have also chosen the random forest method which combines several decision trees and applies the majority voting strategy in order to arrive at an optimal prediction.

**Keywords**: Artificial intelligence, set methods, Random Forest, classifier, prediction, decision tree, unbalanced classes.

# CONTENTS

# GENERAL INTRODUCTION

An accurate and robust decision is usually taken by consensus by a group of decision-makers, rather than by a single person. There are two reasons for putting a group of decision-makers in charge, rather than a single decision-maker: A poor individual decision usually has far-reaching consequences, so we aim for the most objective decision possible by using groups of decision-makers to get several points of view. The second reason for using a committee of decision-makers is that the various stakeholders may have only a partial view of the problem at hand. Agreement on the diagnosis is then reached by majority vote among the various stakeholders.

Machine Learning is currently drawing inspiration from this approach in its search for algorithms for building ensembles of classifiers (Ensemble Learning). The aim is to obtain a new classifier, made up of a set of basic predictors, in such a way as to reduce the number of misclassified examples while maintaining a reasonable computation time.

In the case of unbalanced data, which is quite frequent, the predictor will always tend, during the training phase, to predict individuals from the majority class, and to neglect those from the minority class, which is, moreover, in the majority of cases a class of interest and very interesting. This scenario, which the classifier (predictor) follows i n   t h e   case of class imbalance, exposes it to the constant risk of making biased predictions.

Starting from the behavior of the classifier in front of the preceding situation, we asked ourselves two questions which constitute our problematic namely:

- ➢ How can we deal with dataset imbalance in the case of binary classification?
- ➢ What's the best method to use?

Various methods have been proposed to solve this famous problem. These methods fall into two categories:

- ➢ Methods using sampling strategies are applied at the data level. There are two types: oversampling, where the principle is t o   randomly increase the number of individuals belonging to the minority class in order to rebalance the classes. Sub-sampling, on the other hand, consists in randomly removing individuals from the majority class, in order to achieve balance with the minority class.
- ➢ Algorithmic methods consist in intrinsically modifying
the algorithm to take account of the class imbalance situation.

In our work, we therefore propose both methods in order to identify the best one for unbalanced database problems.

This work, entitled "Decision optimization using ensemblistic methods for the treatment of unbalanced classes", is being carried out over a period running from January 2022 to

December 2022.

A key interest is the prediction of credit card fraud. Our study is limited to setting up a model that combines decision trees to predict credit card fraud detection.

In view of the above, we have divided our work into four chapters, with the exception of the introduction and general conclusion:

➢ Chapter One: We present the state of the art in artificial learning.
➢ Chapter Two: We give a detailed presentation of automatic classifiers and the different types of algorithms used.
➢ Chapter Three: First, we'll look at assembly methods, then at unbalanced classes.
➢ Chapter Four: The final chapter is devoted to a discussion of the experimental results obtained.

# CHAPTER ONE :
# MACHINE LEARNING

## 1. INTRODUCTION

Artificial intelligence (A.I.) is a scientific discipline that studies how to create so-called intelligent programs. By intelligent programs, we generally mean programs capable of solving problems traditionally considered to be specific to human capabilities.

For almost half a century, artificial intelligence researchers have been working on programming machines capable of performing tasks that require intelligence. These include decision support, pattern recognition, process control, prediction, robot control and data mining. Each of these tasks and many others has stimulated the inventiveness of researchers and led to many impressive achievements. However, it is difficult to program machines capable of adapting to all situations and, if necessary, evolving according to new constraints. The challenge is to get around this difficulty by equipping the machine with learning capabilities that enable it to benefit from its experience. This is why research into automatic reasoning has developed alongside research into machine learning.

Before discussing this type of learning, let's take a quick look at some natural learning activities. From birth, a child learns to recognize his mother's smell, then her voice, and more broadly the atmosphere of the place where he lives. Later, he learns to walk, demonstrating a great ability to integrate different signals: sight, sense of balance, motor coordination. He first learns by heart words associated with sounds and their meanings. Later, he learns the rules for distinguishing syllabic groupings within words and pronouncing them. This learning process is long and gradual, requiring repetition and well-chosen sequences of exercises. It is partly supervised by adults, who prepare learning tasks, monitor progress and reward or punish observed results.

In the years that follow, the child gradually learns to master increasingly abstract concepts and operations. Eventually, this time without a teacher to accompany him, he will discover and articulate personal points of view and theories on social, sporting, economic, natural and other phenomena.

## 2. SOME BASIC DEFINITIONS [1]

Before giving a few essential definitions of artificial learning, let's first define two aspects of what learning is.

### 1.1. Learning

➤ In cognitive science, learning is the ability to improve performance as one performs an activity.

➤ It is also seen as a process systematically geared towards acquiring
certain skills, know-how, interpersonal skills and future skills

➤ So, at our level, we can say that learning can also be defined as a process or action aimed at improving abilities (skills, competencies, lucidity, faculties, etc.) as we go along, based on certain observations in the course of some activity.

## 1.2.     Artificial learning

Artificial learning or machine learning can be defined as: A science that seeks and establishes links between the general principles of learning, and the methods and tools that enable learning to take place in a particular context.

A scientific discipline concerned with the development, analysis and implementation of automatable methods that enable a machine (in the broadest sense) to evolve through a learning process, and thus perform tasks that are difficult or impossible to accomplish by more conventional algorithmic means.

Artificial learning, as we shall see later, is a tool capable of solving many problems, and is applied in many fields. It is itself a discipline at the intersection of several others, as shown in the figure below.

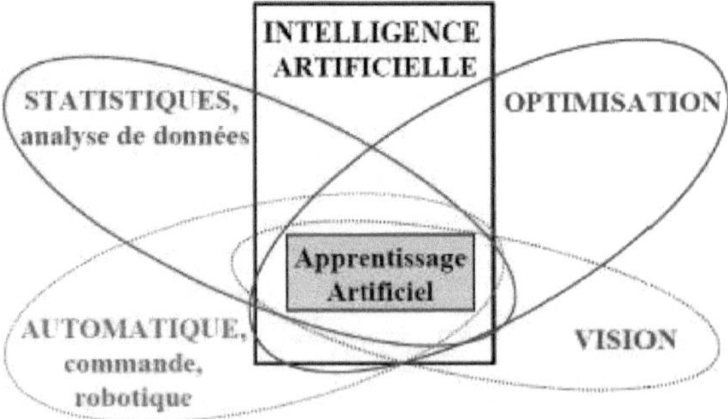


*Figure 1.1: The multidisciplinary nature of artificial learning*

Machine Learning, as it is commonly known, is concerned with writing computer programs capable of automatically improving themselves over time, either on the basis of their own experience, or from previous data provided by other programs.

## 3.   KEY TERMS [18]

Machine Learning systems learn how to combine inputs to formulate effective predictions on data that has never been observed before.

## 1.3. An individual

An individual is the constituent of a set, represented by its studied characteristics. In the following, we will refer to each $x_i \in X$ as an individual. With $X$ : Set of individuals.

## 1.4. A variable

A variable is a function whose purpose is to assign a given value to each individual in the observation domain.
$yh{:}X{\rightarrow}Oh\ xi{:}{\rightarrow}yh(xi)$
With : X : Set of individuals or instances
$Oh$: Observation area.

## 1.5. A label

A label is the result of the prediction; the variable y in a simple linear regression.

## 1.6. A characteristic

A feature is an input variable. A simple Machine Learning project may use a single feature, while a more sophisticated project will use several million, specified in the form: $\{x_1,x_2,...x_n\}$

## 1.7. An example

An example is a particular data instance, x. (x represents a vector.) Examples fall into two categories:

➢ Labeled examples: A labeled example includes one or more features and the label. Labeled examples are used to train the model.
➢ Examples without labels: A label-free example contains features, but not labels, and is used to predict the label on examples t h a t  lack them.

## 1.8. A model

A model defines the relationship between features and the label. It has two life cycle phases:

➢ Learning consists in creating or training the model. In other words, you present the model with labeled examples, and allow it to gradually learn the relationships between the features and the label.
➢ Inference involves applying the trained model to unlabeled examples. In other words, you use the trained model to make effective predictions.

## 1.9. A set of data

A data set is a set of examples already processed, such as for
For each input, its output is known.

$$\beta = \{(xi, yi) \in \{1,...,N\} \mid xi \in X, yi \in Y\}$$

## 1.10.        The difference between regression and classification

Regression models predict continuous values. For example, they formulate predictions that answer questions such as :

> What is the value of a home in Kinshasa?
> What is the probability that a user will click on this ad?

Classification models predict discrete values. For example, they formulate predictions that answer questions such as:

> Is a given e-mail considered spam or not?
> Does this picture represent a dog, a cat or a hamster?

# 4.     THE OBJECTIVES OF MACHINE LEARNING [23]

Machine learning, one of the sub-fields of artificial intelligence, aims to automatically extract and exploit information present in a dataset. In this respect, it covers a vast field of objectives, such as data mining, unsupervised classification, variable selection, discrimination, regression, model selection, rule generation and inference, etc.

It is also highly multidisciplinary: depending on the data and objectives, machine learning calls on computer science, neuroscience, signal processing, cognitive science, information theory, biology, statistics and common sense.

# 5.     THE RISKS OF ARTIFICIAL LEARNING [1].

Among the main characteristics and skills adopted b y  learning
artificial, we can list :

> Training is often synonymous w i t h  learning.
defined above ;

> **Adaptation or improvement**: is the willingness of the model (algorithm or system) to correct its behaviour or to rework its response (e.g. prediction) to new situations;
> **Generalization**: the ability to recognize new, never-before-seen examples
previously ;
> **Intelligibility**: Improving the understanding of learning results, so that the model can provide clear and comprehensible knowledge, in the sense of Comprehensibility or Understandability;
> **Accuracy**: the difference between a value measured or predicted by the model and

an actual value;

➢ **Prediction**: consists in predicting (or telling in advance) the consequences of a present event or decision based on past facts;

➢ **Classification**: In data analysis, classification involves grouping sets of examples, often in an unsupervised way, into classes. These classes are generally organized into a structure known as clusters, or clustering, where classification also involves classifying individuals according to some of their similar characteristics. More broadly, we can also say that classification or cluster analysis (clustering) is the task of segmenting a heterogeneous population into a number of more homogeneous classes called clusters;

➢ **Classification**: refers to the process of recognizing classes described in extension (by the values of their descriptors) in intension (by their properties);

➢ **A classifier**: classifies samples with similar properties, measured on observations, into groups (classes). A linear classifier is a particular type of classifier, which calculates the decision by linear combination of samples;

➢ **Regression**: is a set of statistical methods widely used to analyze the relationship of a variable to one or more other variables.

## 6.  ARTIFICIAL LEARNING CONCEPTS [16]

*Machine learning* seeks to enable computers to mimic the human ability to learn from examples, giving them the ability to act without being explicitly programmed. In general, this field focuses on algorithms that learn from examples and then generalize to new, previously unobserved examples.

Machine learning is now an important component of many fields, such as automatic natural language processing, object recognition, speech recognition, bioinformatics and many others. In 1997, Professor Tom Mitchell of Carnegie Mellon University formally defined machine learning as follows:

Machine learning can be divided into several types, distinguished by the nature of the tasks to be learned. We will now look at the main types of learning.

### 1.11.  SUPPRESSED LEARNING [1] [20]

*A.*  *Introduction*

The aim of supervised learning is to create an intelligent machine capable of predicting the class of a new instance. It exploits algorithms for assigning individuals to their respective classes and these algorithms are called classifiers, defined as an algorithm or mathematical model that assigns or predicts the class of a new instance.

Typically, the aim of a machine learning model is to generate a prediction function $f(\mathbf{x})$ from a supplied data set $D$, known as the training set. In supervised learning, $D$ is made up of pairs of examples $(\mathbf{x}, \mathbf{y})$, where $\mathbf{x}$ **is** a vector serving as input to the model and $\mathbf{y}$ is a target vector representing what is to be predicted. Note that inputs and targets are presented as vectors, but could be replaced by scalars. Having a target for each example, and using it, is the key feature of supervised learning. Suppose the function $f(\mathbf{x})$, taking as input the vector $\mathbf{x}$ of size $J$, has the following form:

$$f(x) = \theta_0 + \theta_1 x_1 + \theta_2 x_2 + \dots + \theta_J x_J \ (1.1)$$

Where $\theta_0$ to $\theta_J$ are the parameters of the learning model. The aim of this model is therefore to find the parameter values to obtain the best possible predictions, i.e. as close as possible to the targets.

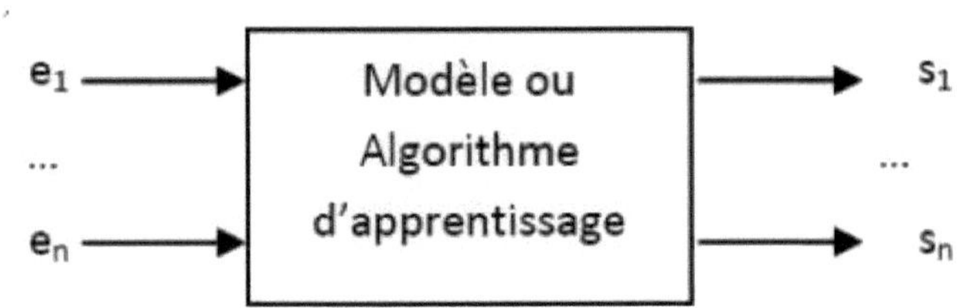


*Figure 1.2: Supervised model diagram*

**B.**      <u>*Formalism*</u>

Given that we start with examples and end up classifying individuals, we're in the process of induction, i.e. generalization. We need to take into account the fact that we make mistakes in this process. That's why we need to minimize the risk of false assignments at classifier level.

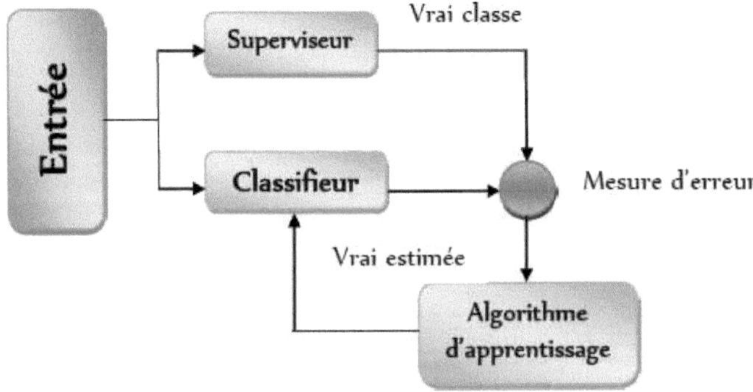


*Figure 1.3: Supervised learning*

**C.**      <u>*Some algorithms that can be used for this analysis*</u>

Several classification algorithms have been developed in the field of supervised learning. We present some of these approaches here.

➢      <u>*Decision tree*</u>

The decision tree, as its name suggests, is a grouping of local functions structured in the form of a tree. In fact, the functions are usually sufficiently localized to be simple condition-action rules. The root node is associated with a subset D. A node is either a leaf, or an internal node using a function f to separate its associated set D between at least two children. Each node in the tree thus represents a simplified classifier that makes its decision based on a minimum of features.

Decision trees are also techniques for both supervised and unsupervised learning, enabling the graphical representation of a classification procedure. They are also powerful and popular tools for classification and prediction. These decision trees enable learning by either establishing new connections or modifying existing ones. Based on known problem data, they can be used to predict by reducing the solution domain level by level.

The basic idea behind decision tree learning is to recursively divide the examples in the training set as efficiently as possible, using a function f that minimizes the empirical error of this local classification, until subsets of examples are obtained that contain (almost) only examples that all belong to the same class.

> ***K nearest neighbors***

The k nearest neighbor method is a supervised learning method. Abbreviated k-NN or KNN, from k-nearest neighbors. In this context, we have a

training database made up of N "input-output" pairs. To estimate the output associated with a new input x, the k-nearest-neighbor method consists in taking into account (in an identical way) the k training samples whose input is closest to the new input x, according to a distance to be defined. A particular feature of k-NN algorithms is that they are particularly sensitive to the local structure of the data.

> ***Neural networks***

Neural networks are a set of interconnected neurons (processor or computational unit) such that each neuron calculates the weighted sum of its inputs and assigns the activation function to this sum, so that the result obtained is sent to downstream neurons. As learning systems, neural networks implement the principle of induction, i.e. learning from experience. This means adjusting the synaptic weights of each network unit in such a way that when a new individual arrives, all we have to do is subject it to the network, and we have the predicted output, i.e. the class to which it belongs.

> ***Support vector machines***

Support Vector Machines are a recent method of classification by supervised learning, introduced by Vladimir Vapnik in 1995. The rise in popularity of this method is justified by its solid theoretical underpinnings. This method is based on the existence of a linear separator in an appropriate space and the use of a kernel function, which enable optimal data separation.

The aim of SVMs, in the case of a binary classification problem, is to construct a decision function (separator) that allows us to better separate the data and maximize the distance between two classes.

## 1.12.  UNSUPERVISED LEARNING [16] [20]

The aim of unsupervised learning is to create homogeneous classes from an unlabeled heterogeneous population (i.e. we don't have the assumptions or additional information about the data). These classes are created using automatic classification algorithms, also known as clustering.

Unlike the supervised approach, the dataset $D$ used in unsupervised learning is not composed of pairs of examples $(\mathbf{x}, \mathbf{y})$, but only of $\mathbf{x}$, i.e. there is no longer a target associated with each example. In such a framework, a machine learning model will model the information provided as input only.

In the unsupervised approach, the function $f(\mathbf{x})$ returned by a learning algorithm is not dictated by the nature of the data. Indeed, unlike the supervised approach, there is no goal explicitly expressed through targets.

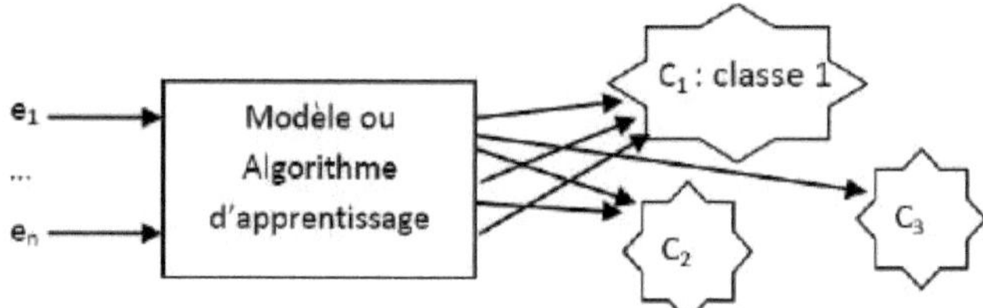


*Figure 1.4: Unsupervised model diagram*

There are many problems in unsupervised learning. Here is a list of the most common:

➢ **Feature extraction:** The learned function $f(\mathbf{x})$ provides a new representation for the input $\mathbf{x}$. In general, this representation is used to perform another task for which it is more useful than the original input.
➢ **Density estimation:** Here $f(\mathbf{x})$ must estimate the probability distribution of the examples.
of the drive assembly.
➢ *Clustering*: In the space containing the training set data, the learning algorithm must identify clusters of distinct examples. The result is a function $f(\mathbf{x})$, which provides the clustering index associated with example $\mathbf{x}$.
➢ **Dimensionality reduction:** As with feature extraction, $f(\mathbf{x})$ needs to provide a new representation for the input $\mathbf{x}$. However, the aim this time is to obtain a representation with a

smaller dimensionality than that of the input, while retaining the important information.

The clustering process relies on a precise measure of the similarity of the objects to be grouped. This measure is called distance or metric. There are several different clustering algorithms, such as :

➢        K-means (KMeans): KMeans is an algorithm for partitioning data into K number of groups or clusters. Each object is associated with a single cluster. The K number is set by the user.
➢        Fuzzy KMeans. This is a variant of the previous algorithm, which proposes that an object
is not associated with just one group.
➢        Expectation-Maximization (EM). This algorithm uses probabilities to describe that an object belongs to a group. The center of the group is then recalculated with respect to the average of the probabilities of each object in the group.
➢        Hierarchical clustering. Two sub-algorithms are derived from this: on the one hand, the
On the one hand, there's the "bottom up" approach, whose function is to agglomerate similar groups, thus reducing their number (making them more legible) and proposing a hierarchical order, and on the other, the "top down" approach, which does the opposite by recursively dividing the first group into subsets.

## 1.13.        SEMI-SUPERVISED LEARNING [16]

Semi-supervised learning is in fact a mixture of the two approaches we have just presented, i.e. supervised and unsupervised learning. Why use both types of learning together? The answer lies in the data. Indeed, it's important to realize that it's not always easy to obtain labeled data, i.e. a training set where each example is linked to a target. Often, the size of the training set is not large enough to adequately represent the distribution of the data and thus allow for adequate generalization to new examples. Lack of labeled data for certain tasks is not uncommon. This shortage is due to the fact that specialized people are sometimes required to associate targets by hand, which can prove too time-consuming or costly.

To compensate for the lack of labeled data, we can also use unlabeled sets, which are usually easier to generate and therefore much more numerous. Usually, a semi-supervised learning algorithm will start by using unlabeled data for density estimation. This first step is used to initialize the model parameters and thus capture some information about the data distribution. We then continue with the same model, performing supervised learning on the labeled training set.

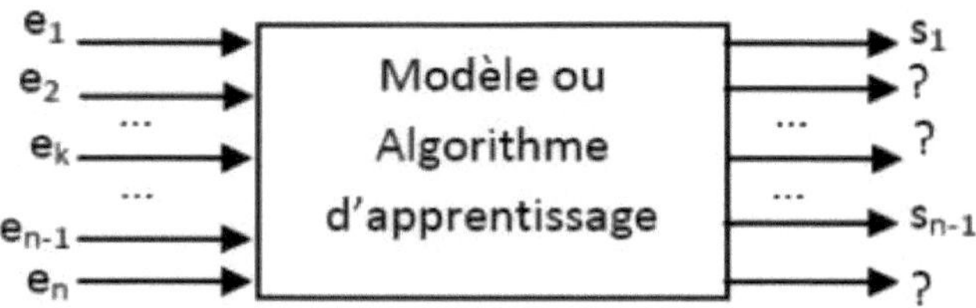


*Figure 1.5: Semi-supervised model diagram*

In the end, a learning algorithm will provide a function $f(\mathbf{x})$ that predicts the targets of the labeled data. This approach is particularly effective when we have a small number of labeled examples and a large number of unlabeled examples.

## 1.14.    REINFORCEMENT LEARNING [16]

The field of reinforcement learning seeks to teach an agent to behave in the right way within a specific environment, i.e. in such a way as to achieve a goal chosen in advance by the user. The problem to be solved is divided into a sequence of steps. At each step, an agent must choose from a set of actions, enabling it to interact with its environment. Unlike supervised learning, there is no target that gives the agent the opportunity to learn a behavior. Instead, the agent receives a user-determined signal that lets it know whether it has acted correctly.

For each step in the sequence, the agent receives information about its environment that will help it choose the appropriate action. During learning, the agent will seek to maximize the number of positive signals in order to improve its behavior.

## 7.    THE BENEFITS OF ARTIFICIAL LEARNING [1]

Traditional analytical tools are not powerful enough to fully exploit the value of Big Data. The volume of data is too large for comprehensive analysis, and the correlations and relationships between data are too great for analysts to test all hypotheses to derive value from the data. Basic analytical methods are used by business intelligence and reporting tools to report sums, make up accounts and perform SQL queries. On-line analytical processing is a systematized extension of these basic analytical tools, requiring human intervention to specify what is to be calculated.

The contributions of this field can be grouped into two main areas: data mining and knowledge extraction and pattern recognition. Here are just a few of the contributions we can attribute to artificial learning:

➢    Predict or forecast customer behavior;
➢    Analyzes company data to help them better target their advertising campaigns or offer better service;
➢    Recognizing and interpreting human speech;

➤        Automatically analyzes satellite photos to detect certain terrestrial resources;

➤        Assists experts in making decisions in complex and changing environments, such as the financial market or medical diagnostics;

➤        Search immense heterogeneous databases, like the millions of Web pages accessible to all.

## 8.      FIELD OF APPLICATION [17]

Let's take a look at how to make a program more efficient by giving it the ability to learn. Let's take a look at some of the applications of artificial intelligence:

➤        A speech recognition program increases its performance the more it is used by the same person: this is an experience that is easy to put into practice today if you buy personal voice dictation software.

➤        A terrestrial resource detection program learns to recognize an area of pollution in the middle of the sea, from a database of example images of areas known to be clean or polluted: this database is used as an experiment to determine its decision on an unknown area.

➤        A diagnostic program based on a set of evolving information taken from a patient must have been provided with knowledge, based on practitioner and expert diagnoses of typical situations.

➤        Web search engines could be equipped with a module for adapting to the user's browsing style: this is a desirable feature to enhance their usability.

➤        The exploitation of a company's customer files is often carried out by an expert or an expert program which uses explicit rules to target a customer segment likely to be interested in a new product. But these rules can also be acquired automatically, through a learning process whose aim is to provide new expert knowledge that is both effective and intelligible to the expert.

➤        A chess program is generally very efficient a priori; but it's natural to try to equip it with a module where it can analyze its defeats and victories, to improve its average performance in future games.

## 9.      THE GOAL [1]

Artificial learning aims to train an algorithm based on examples, with the aim of building a predictive model. In other words, the aim is to be able to determine what links an output to an input.

Thus, the aim of artificial sciences, and in particular artificial learning, is to understand natural phenomena, but this understanding must involve the construction of models that are capable of performing simulations.

## 10.    SUMMARY

In this introductory chapter we have attempted to describe the environment in which we work, and the context of artificial learning, which is one of the sub-domains of artificial intelligence, and aims to automatically extract and exploit information present in a dataset.

We have succinctly developed the field of artificial learning, while touching on virtually all related aspects such as fields of application, features and a few methods. It illustrates a cross-sectional view of the whole work, so that we have almost touched lightly on the generalities of the concepts in the remainder of the chapters.

Now that the objectives set for this chapter have been achieved, we'll move on in the next chapter to the notion of the automatic classifier, which is the systematic division into classes of concepts with common characteristics, in order to facilitate their study.

# CHAPTER TWO :
# AUTOMATIC CLASSIFIERS

## 1.    INTRODUCTION [11]

In many fields (medicine, economics, biology, etc.), the development of information technology (hardware and software) has made it possible to store and manage large volumes of data. But unfortunately, when this volume of data is considerable, it is difficult to derive useful information from it, because the sheer volume of data obscures the knowledge that is useful for decision-making. Data mining methods have been developed to overcome this difficulty.

The automatic classification problem can be described as follows: a set of data, each observation of which is made up of a target variable, the variable we are seeking to classify, and explanatory variables, which may be used to predict the behavior of the target variable. In the context of a classification problem, the target variable must be categorical, each of the values it can take being called a class.

## 2.    SOME DEFINITIONS [23] [32]

The Trésor de la Langue Française defines classification as "the systematic division into classes or categories of beings, things or concepts having common characteristics, in particular in order to facilitate their study".

We therefore define a classifier as an automatic tool. From a mathematical point of view, a classifier is an application of an attribute space X (discrete or continuous) to a set of labels Y.

## 3.    THE GOAL [20]

The aim of classification is to establish order relationships between individuals, in order to obtain the most concise information possible, reaching the highest level of abstraction.

## 4.    CLASSIFICATION TECHNIQUES [20]

Automatic classification techniques produce groupings of objects (or individuals) described by a number of variables or characters (attributes). The use of such techniques is often linked to assumptions, if not requirements, about the groupings of individuals. There are several families of classification algorithms, such as : Partitioning algorithms; Bottom-up (agglomerative) algorithms; Top-down (divisive) algorithms.

Each of these techniques has its own advantages and disadvantages, which are why they are selected according to the application context. Of course, these aspects also justify the combined use of classifiers.

# 5.  CLASSIFICATION METHODS [11][12][21][25][29]

The problem of classification consists in assigning the objects in a data set to predefined categories or classes. This type of question is one of the problems encountered during the data grouping and classification phase.

In this respect, no single classification method can be specified for any particular problem. We will present an overview of the best-known classification methods, which can be divided into two groups:

➢        Automatic classification methods (also known as clustering methods): methods based on the notion of unsupervised learning, which involves grouping objects belonging to a set T into restricted classes in such a way that objects in the same class are dispersed as little as possible.

➢        Assignment methods (also known as "classifiers") based on the notion of supervised learning: methods using a set of examples in which the membership classes are known in advance. From this set, assignment norms (or rules) are defined.

## a.        AUTOMATIC CLASSIFICATION METHODS

The aim of these methods is to group individuals into a limited number of homogeneous classes. In this type of method, classes are obtained using formalized algorithms. We also distinguish between non-hierarchical and hierarchical classification methods.

### *A.        <u>Non-hierarchical methods</u>*

These are methods that directly produce a partition into a fixed number of classes. These methods include :

### i.<u>Leadership method</u>

This method considers each object only once. When the first object arrives, it is assigned the first class and becomes its leader. Then, each time a new object arrives, we calculate its distance from the leaders of each of the classes existing at that moment, and compare this distance with a threshold.

If this distance is less than the set threshold, the new object is assigned the class of the first leader found (for which the calculated distance is less than the threshold), otherwise a new class is created and the new object becomes the leader of this class.

➢        <u>k-means method</u>

This method is also known as the moving center algorithm. In this type of algorithm, the class is represented by its center of gravity. The k-means algorithm developed by McQueen in 1967 is one of the best-known clustering algorithms. It is based on the centroid method.

*B.*        *Hierarchical methods*

Hierarchical classification consists of grouping objects or groups of objects into progressively finer classes, aggregating the closest objects at each stage. It thus provides a set of partitions of the set of objects.

This approach uses the notion of distance to reflect the homogeneity or heterogeneity of classes. Thus, an element is considered to belong to a class if it is closer to that class than to all the others.

➤         **Inductive learning methods**

Inductive learning methods involve inferring decision rules from examples of different classes. This is done with the aim of generalizing to predict new cases, based on the parameters describing them.

➤         **k-nearest neighbor method (k-ppv)**

The general principle of the k-ppv method is to search the training set T, containing all the individuals and their assignment classes, for a number k of the closest possible individuals to the individual to be classified. The individual is then assigned to the majority class among the k individuals found. The number k is set a priori by the user.

➤         **Neural networks**

Neural networks are a set of interconnected neurons (processor or computational unit) such that each neuron calculates the weighted sum of its inputs and assigns the activation function to this sum, so that the result obtained is sent to downstream neurons. It is based on the human brain paradigm, as shown in the figure below:

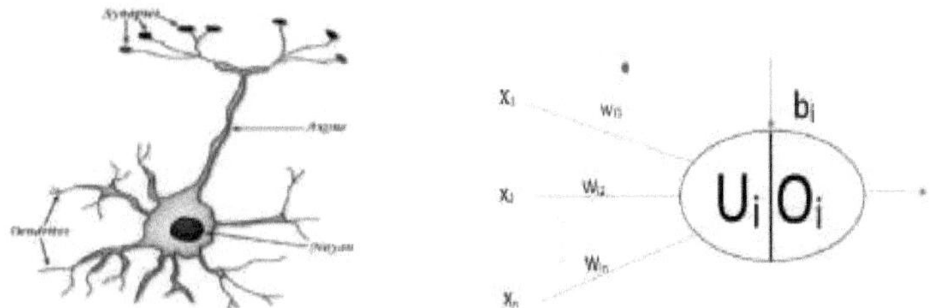


*Figure 2.1: Biological and formal neuron*

The brain is made up of around 1012 neurons (trillion), with 1000 to 10000 synapses (connections) per neuron. The neuron is a cell composed of a cell body and a nucleus. The cell body branches to form what are known as dendrites. These are sometimes so numerous that they are referred to as dendritic hairs or dendritic arborization. It is via the dendrites that information is conveyed from the outside to the soma, the neuron's body.



➢ **<u>Support vector machines</u>**

Support Vector Machines are a recent method of classification by supervised learning, introduced by Vladimir Vapnik in 1995. The rise in popularity of this method is justified by its solid theoretical underpinnings. This method is based on the existence of a linear separator in an appropriate space and the use of a kernel function, which enable optimal data separation.

**Operating principle : The** aim of SVMs, in the case of a binary classification problem, is to construct a decision function (separator) that allows us to better separate the data and maximize the distance between two classes.

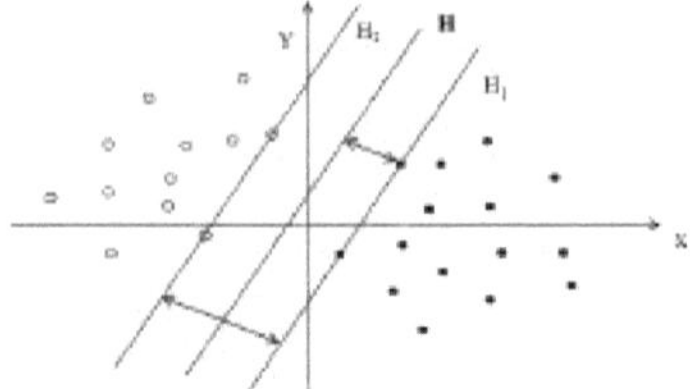

*Figure 2.2: Support vector machine*

➢ **<u>Assignment using the decision tree approach</u>**

**Principle:** A decision tree is a simple recursive structure used to express a sequential classification process in which a match is established between an object described by a set of characteristics (attributes), and a set of disjoint classes. Each leaf of the tree denotes a class, and each interior node a test on one or more attributes, producing a decision sub-tree for each possible test result.

**Decision tree construction:** Given a training set $T = \{(x_i, c_j) / i = 1,$
..., m; j=1, ..., k}. The idea behind building a decision tree using T is to refine T into successive subsets leading to collections of objects with at most one class. To do this, we choose a test involving one or more results $\{R_1, R_2, ..., R_L\}$.

T is then partitioned into subsets $T_1, T_2, ..., T_L$ where $T_i$ contains all the individuals in T with the result $R_i$ for the chosen test. The resulting tree consists of a decision node identifying the test and a branch for each possible result.

The most important step in building decision trees is choosing the best test. This minimizes the mixing of classes within each subset created by the test. The selection criterion most often used is based on Shannon's information theory. This type of criterion is used to select the various tests using the entropy gain criterion. To obtain a simpler, more precise tree for classifying new cases, we can apply the pruning principle.

The aim of this principle is to improve the tree's generalization and prediction qualities. The pruning principle consists in deleting parts of the tree deemed unnecessary (or inefficient for predicting the class of new cases).

**Assigning new individuals:** The rule for assigning a new individual is as follows: Starting from the tree root, the individual moves down the tree until it reaches a leaf. If the leaf represents a single class, the individual is assigned to that class. If the leaf represents a mixture of classes, the individual is assigned to the majority class.

## 6. THE PERFORMANCE OF CLASSIFICATION METHODS

Most of the classification methods mentioned in this chapter have been widely applied in many fields, including decision-making problems. The question is: how can we evaluate the performance of a classification method? In general, we divide the available data set into two subsets: one for learning and the other for testing.

The training set is used to determine the parameters of the classification model, such as the weights in the case of a neural network. The test set is used to test the performance of the method by calculating the rate of correct classification of the set of cases. This rate is determined by dividing the number of correctly classified cases by the number of cases tested.

## 7. SUMMARY

In this chapter, we have presented three classification techniques: partitioning algorithms, bottom-up algorithms and top-down algorithms. These techniques are the most widely used in the literature.

We have also cited the various classification methods proposed in the literature to deal with the problem of classifying unbalanced data. They are grouped into three main families: hierarchical methods, non-hierarchical methods and assignment methods.

In the next chapter, we propose one of the automatic classification methods that can be used to tackle the problem of classifying unbalanced data.

# CHAPTER THREE :
## SET METHODS AND CLASSES

## UNBALANCED

## 1. THE AUTOMATIC CLASSIFIER [2][12][18][22][25].

### 1.1. INTRODUCTION

Ensemble methods are a family or set o f  algorithms that generate a collection of classifiers and aggregate their predictions. In the literature, various approaches have been proposed to achieve higher-performance classification, including ensemble methods.

### 1.2. OBJECTIVES OF THE ASSEMBLY APPROACH

The aim is for the final predictor to be better than each of the individual predictors. Instead of trying to optimize one method, assembly methods generate several prediction rules and then pool their different answers.

### 1.3. DEFINITIONS OF ASSEMBLY METHODS

According to Dietterich, an ensemblistic method is a diverse but precise set of classifications whose decisions are combined by averaging or voting (the most popular decision) to give a more precise decision.

A classifier is accurate if its error rate is lower than a random classification, and two classifications are diverse if they make different errors on new data. Note that these methods can be applied to all unstable algorithms, those for which a small change in the training data induces a large change in the final classifier.

### 1.4. IMPROVING PRECISION

A set of classifiers is more accurate than a single classifier for the following reasons: since classifiers are diverse, they make mistakes in different places, and taking an average decision or a vote of their individual decisions reduces the risk of making the wrong decision.

### 1.5. TYPES OF CLASSIFICATION METHODS

#### A.  *Bagging*

Bagging is an ensemble method based on the concepts of bootstrapping and aggregating. Bootstrapping is designed to randomly and remotely generate L independent copies of S objects, called bootstrap, from the initial set of S-sized training samples.

An object in the initial database can be selected several times, just as it can be absent from the generated copies. The same classifier is learned on each copy. This results in L classifiers with different performances.

Aggregation consists of combining these classifiers, using majority voting as the combination rule. The following algorithm illustrates how bagging works.

Algorithm 1: The Bagging method

**Entrance :**
$B^a$ : learning base
S: learning base size
X: shape to be recognized L classifier
**Start**
**For** j from 1 to L **do Start**
Generate sub-base $_{bj}$ from $B^a$
Construct the classifier $_{ej}$ (x) using the basis $_{bj}$
**End for**
Combine the L classifiers built by majority voting to obtain the final decision
of x.
**End**

Bagging is generally a technique for improving the performance of unstable classifiers (neural networks, decision trees, etc.). For stable classifiers (k nearest neighbors with large k, linear regression), it deteriorates the performance of the combination. The final bagging prediction is obtained by majority vote among the intermediate classifiers.

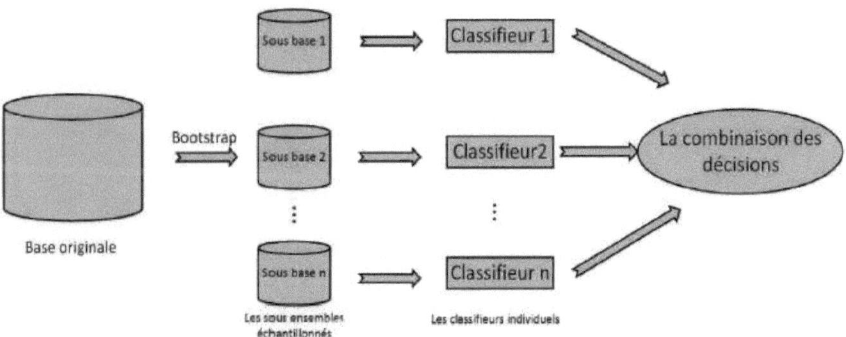


*Figure 3.1: Bagging principle*

**_B._**        **_Boosting_**

Boosting is an ensemble method, the aim of which is to improve results and obtain a better classifier from an underperforming one. The principle is based on the combination of classifiers.

Unlike bagging, where bootstrap training sets and classifiers are built independently, in boosting the training samples are built incrementally by the same classifier and sequentially. Initially, all training samples have equal weights and the classifier is built on this basis. Then, for each step, the samples are weighted so that misclassified objects have high weights, and the classifier is run on the new, weighted training set. In this way, we finally obtain a set of classifiers which are combined by a weighted vote to reach the final decision.

Algorithm 2: The Boosting Method

---

**Input**: Xapp: set of learning examples
**For** each example $_{xi} \in$ Xapp **do**
$_{wi} \leftarrow$ 1=N
**End for**
**For** t ε {1,... , T} **do**
$_{Ct} \leftarrow$ workbook built with these N examples weighted by the $_{wi}$
$_{and} \leftarrow$ Ct error measured on this set of examples with this weighting
$\beta t \leftarrow 1/2\ log(_{1\text{-}et/et})$
**For** each example xi $\in$ Xapp **do**
wi $\leftarrow wie\text{-}\beta tyiyCt(xi)$
**End for**
Normalize weights (so that their sum equals 1)
**End for**

---

Boosting is based on the same principle as Bagging: it builds a set of classifiers which are then aggregated by a weighted average of the results. However, in the case of Boosting, this set of classifiers is built in a recurrent and iterative way. In other words, each classifier is an adaptive version of the previous one, giving more weight to poorly predicted observations.

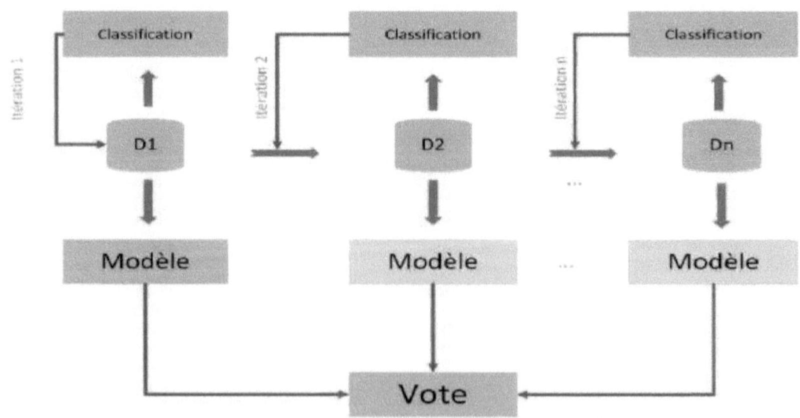


*Figure 3.2: Boosting principle*

30

*C.*        ***Random forests* [10]**

Decision tree forests (also known as random forests or random forest classifiers) are part of the world of machine learning. They combine the concepts of random subspaces and bagging. The decision tree forest algorithm performs training on multiple decision trees trained on slightly different subsets of data.

A very interesting extension of decision trees was proposed by Breiman with random forests, which are a bagging of random decision trees (each tree is built on a subset of variables, drawn randomly).

Random forests are composed (as the term "forest" implies) of a set of decision trees. These trees are distinguished from each other by the sub-sample of data on which they are trained. These sub-samples are drawn at random (hence the term "random") from the medical dataset.

Random forests are ensemble methods based on random injection. The general principle of ensemble methods is to build a collection of predictors, and then aggregate all their predictions. In a classification framework, aggregation amounts, for example, to a majority vote among the classes provided by the predictors.

Chen et Al have proposed two methods for using random forests on unbalanced datasets which are :

The first is called Balanced Random Forest (BRF), and involves bootstrapping the minority class, then drawing the same number of individuals from the majority class (with a discount). In this way, the sample for each tree is balanced.

The balanced random forest is used when data learning is extremely unbalanced, and there is a significant probability that a bootstrap sample will contain little or no minority class, resulting in a tree that performs poorly in predicting the minority class.

The balanced random forest algorithm is illustrated below:

➤        For each iteration in the random forest, draw a bootstrap sample of the minority class. Randomly draw the same number of cases, with replacement, from the majority class.
➤        Specify a classification tree for the data at maximum size, without pruning. The tree is induced with algorithm C4, 5, with the following modification: At each node, instead of searching all variables for the optimal split, search only a randomly chosen set of variables.
➤        Repeat the above two steps for the desired number of times. Aggregate the set predictions and make the final prediction.

The second approach, called Weighted Random Forest (WBF), simply involves building cost-sensitive trees. Both approaches deliver good results without the added complexity of conventional random forests.

Weighted Random Forest is another approach to making Random Forest more suitable for learning from extremely unbalanced data, following the idea of cost-sensitive learning. Since the Random Forest classifier tends to be biased in favor of the majority class, we will impose a heavier penalty for misclassifying the minority class. We assign a weight to each class, with the minority class receiving a higher weight (i.e., a higher misclassification cost).

The final class prediction for WRF is then determined by aggregating the weighted vote of each individual tree, where the weights are average weights in the terminal nodes. Class weights are an essential tuning parameter for achieving the desired performance. Accuracy estimation from RF can be used to select weights.

*Table 3.1: Parallelism between three classifiers*

| Comparative topics | Boosting | Bagging | Random Forest |
|---|---|---|---|
| Final prediction | The final prediction is the result of a combination (weighted vote) of several predictions<br><br>or by the mean of the predictors. | The final prediction for a new example is obtained by : Majority vote (classification)<br><br>Average prediction (regression) | In regression mode, the final prediction is then In classification mode, aggregation consists of to make a vote<br><br>majority among class labels provided by predictors |
| Advantage | Good prediction performance<br>Does not require large trees Importance of variables<br>Fast, simple and easy to implement | Bagging reduces variance when predictors are unstable Estimation of prediction error by Bootstrap.<br>Easy to set up and adaptable to any method learning | Well suited to very large dimensions Very simple to implement They are generally more effective than simple decision trees. |
| Disadvantage | Problem if outliers or noisy points, exaggerated weights Deployment of such a model remains complicated | Important calculation for evaluating a large number of classifiers. Need to store all models in the combination to evaluate a new example The final model is not easily interpretable | Have the disadvantage of being more difficult to interpret Often take a long time to learn Extreme values often poorly estimated in regression cases |

# 2. UNBALANCED CLASSES [12][18][20][25]

## 2.1. INTRODUCTION

Most learning systems assume that all the datasets used for learning are balanced. However, in real-life applications, this balance is not always verified. Handling classes from unbalanced data is a classic but still largely open problem in data mining, especially as it is widely used in many fields. Imbalance in datasets can be as high as 1 in 100, 1 in 1000, 1 in 10,000 and often even higher.

Indeed, if, for example, 99% of the data belong to a single class, it will be difficult to do better than the 1% error obtained by classifying all the individuals in this class. We therefore need to find other solutions and hypotheses adapted to the imbalance problem, without calling into question the fundamentals of the algorithms. In this chapter, we present the various problems associated with class asymmetry and summarize the approaches proposed to deal with the problem of imbalance in learning.

## 2.2. PROBLEMS ASSOCIATED WITH UNBALANCED DATA

In a two-class classification problem, the training data of the majority class is far greater in number than that of the minority class. All algorithms designed to achieve a minimum error rate will always tend to neglect the minority class, which is in the majority of cases the most interesting, because of this disproportion. This justifies the strong link between the two forms of asymmetry in supervised learning. In fact, asymmetry takes two main forms: class imbalance and cost asymmetry. Class imbalance concerns problems where one of the modalities of the target variable is much less represented than the others, which disturbs the learning algorithms. Cost asymmetry refers to cases where error costs are not symmetrical.

It is proposed to distinguish six categories of data-related problems
and learning rare classes. These categories are :

➢　　　　Absolute" lack of data: this problem arises when there isn't enough data available to clearly define class boundaries. This is the main problem of imbalance. Figure (III.3) illustrates this problem: the observations in red are not sufficient to clearly define the concept of this class.

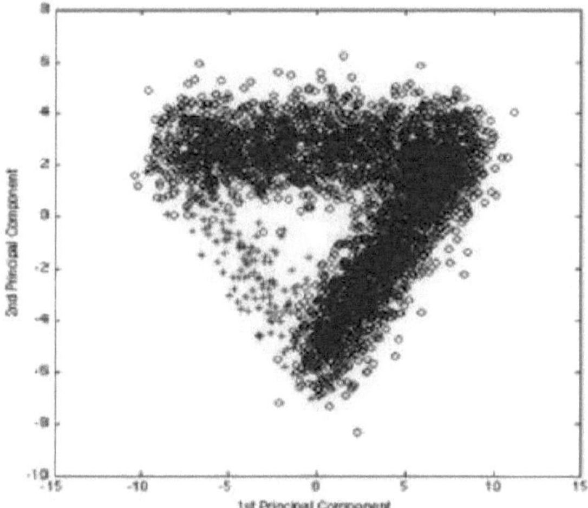

*Figure 3.3: Absolute lack of data*

➢ Relative" lack of data: this problem is similar to the absolute lack of data, except that

that in this case the lack is relative to the size of the majority database. The observations of the minority class are not rare in an absolute sense, but are much less represented than those of the other class (majority class). As shown in figure (III.4), objects from the minority class (in red) are represented in the data with a proportion of 50% compared with objects from the majority class (in blue).

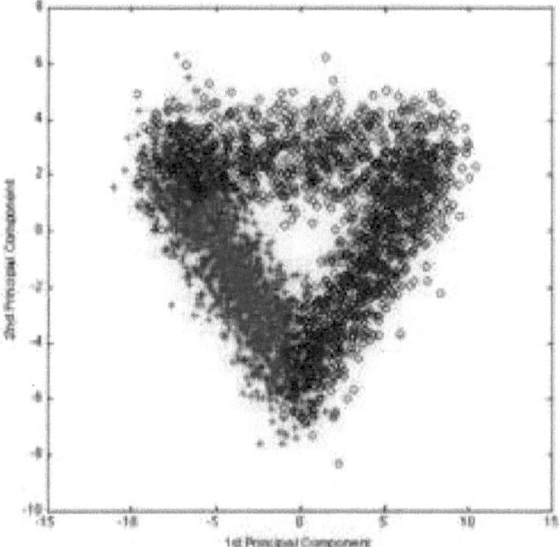

*Figure 3.4: Relative lack of data*

➢ Inappropriate metrics: in this case, the measures used during the learning process and to assess results are not adapted to the problems of unbalanced classes.

➢ Data fragmentation: this problem is linked to top-down algorithms, which start from the space of all individuals and recursively partition it into smaller and smaller subspaces.

➢ Inappropriate induction margin: this is the margin applied to the rule learned on training data for generalization.

➢ Noisy data: noise has a  greater impact on rare classes than on more common classes frequent.

## 2.3.    CLASS-SENSITIVE LEARNING

### A.    *SAMPLING STRATEGIES*

Sampling is an essential technique in statistics and data mining, especially when the class to be predicted is rare. These techniques can be used to adjust the sample in such a way as to increase the frequency of this class or decrease that of the majority classes. All algorithms achieving a minimum error rate will always tend to neglect the minority class, which is the most interesting, because of this disproportion. Sampling techniques provide an effective response to this problem. Among the various sampling techniques available are :

➢ **Sub-sampling**

Subsampling is a way of rebalancing datasets by removing a certain number of individuals belonging to the majority class. This is a simple method, but it runs the risk of removing individuals who are important for the concept of the majority class. To avoid this problem, several techniques have been proposed to guide sub-sampling.

Use the Tomek link as a sub-sampling method. Consider two individuals $x_1$ and $x_2$ belonging respectively to class i and class j, and $d(x_1, x_2)$ the distance between these two individuals. The pair $(x_1, x_2)$ is a Tomek link if there is no individual x3 such that $d(x_3, x_1) < d(x_1, x_2)$ or $d(x_3, x_2) < d(x_1, x_2)$. If these two individuals form a Tomek link, then one of them is noise, or both are boundary points.

➢ **Oversampling**

In contrast to sub-sampling, over-sampling consists in increasing the number of individuals in the minority class. As a first solution, it has been proposed to randomly duplicate the individuals, but this solution risks slowing down the algorithms by adding individuals, while providing models unable to generalize (risk of overlearning).

To avoid these problems, several methods have been proposed: The approach is a technique for generating artificial individuals in the minority class. For each individual in the minority class, its k nearest neighbors in the same class are calculated, then a certain number of them are selected. Artificial individuals are then randomly scattered along the line between the individual in the minority class and its selected neighbors.

*B.*        ***APPROACH TOGETHER***

The ensemble approach is another family of techniques that has been proposed in the literature to deal with the problem of class imbalance. The principle behind these techniques is to make any type of algorithm sensitive to imbalance, in particular by boosting or bagging methods.

Boosting is an iterative algorithm that assigns different weights to the individuals in the training set. After each iteration, the weight on misclassified individuals increases and that on correctly classified individuals decreases. Since errors are often concentrated on rare classes, boosting can be said to improve learning on unbalanced datasets by increasing the weights of individuals belonging to the minority class.

Bagging (Bootstrap aggregating) is based on the principle of modifying the training sample A to create a diversified set of classifiers. This method consists in building each hypothesis from a bootstrap resampling of A, where a bootstrap is the random drawing, with discount, of a sample of size n from an initial sample of the same size. The hypotheses thus constructed are then combined by a majority vote.

A random decision tree bagging (each tree is built on a subset of variables, drawn randomly) known as a random forest was proposed by Breiman. Two methods have been proposed for using random forests on unbalanced datasets. The first, "Balanced Random Forest", involves bootstrapping the minority class, then drawing the same number of individuals from the majority class (with discounting). In this way, the sample for each tree is balanced. The second approach is called "Weighted Random Forest" and consists in building cost-sensitive trees.

We have another sampling strategy, called an algorithmic strategy, which consists in acting at the algorithmic level and not on the training data. These approaches have been proposed to make learning algorithms sensitive to dataset imbalance.

## 3.    COMBINATION OF CLASSIFIERS [13] [25]

### 3.1.    INTRODUCTION

The combination of classifiers seeks to combine information obtained from different systems, with the aim of making inferences from these observations. It i s   analogous to the terminals used by actors to infer knowledge about the external world, so any method of combining classifiers aims to make the most of the complementarity of the individual decision systems involved, which is the challenge of research in this field. The combination method or strategy (also known as decision fusion) is highly dependent on the nature of these classifiers.

Thus, the field of multi-classifier systems (MCS) research, focuses on finding out how several classifiers can be applied to obtain better classification systems. It has been shown that MCS methods can improve the performance of our decision trees to better predict breast cancer.

There are two main avenues of research into MCS systems. The first is concerned with the way individual classifiers are designed, and the second with research into the different types of combinations of these classifiers.

## 3.2. FRONT OF THE SUIT

The main idea behind the combination of classifiers is to increase the performance, several researchers have made the following observations:

> There is no better classifier capable of processing or learning any distribution of training data.
> No classifier can sufficiently and correctly discriminate a large set of classes.
> When several classifiers are used separately for the same data set, the sets of misclassified data are not necessarily the same.

From these observations and many others, the idea emerged of getting classifiers to cooperate in order to increase the performance of the final decision, with two major reasons behind the combination:

> Accuracy: a more reliable decision can be obtained by combining advice (Outputs) of several experts (classifiers).
> Efficiency: a complex problem can be broken down into several sub-problems that are easier to understand and solve (divide and conquer).

## 3.3. CLASSIFIER COMBINATION TYPES

The proliferation of work on combination has led to the development of numerous schemes that process data in different ways. Three approaches to classifier combination can be considered: parallel, sequential and hybrid. Other "looping" or "interacting" schemes are also possible. But despite the diversity of combination schemes, determining the best organization remains an open problem.

### A. *Sequential approach*

Sequential combination, also known as serial combination, is organized in successive levels of decision, gradually reducing the number of possible classes. In each level, there is a single classifier which takes into account the answers provided by the classifier placed upstream in order to process the rejections or confirm the decision obtained on the form presented to it in this figure :

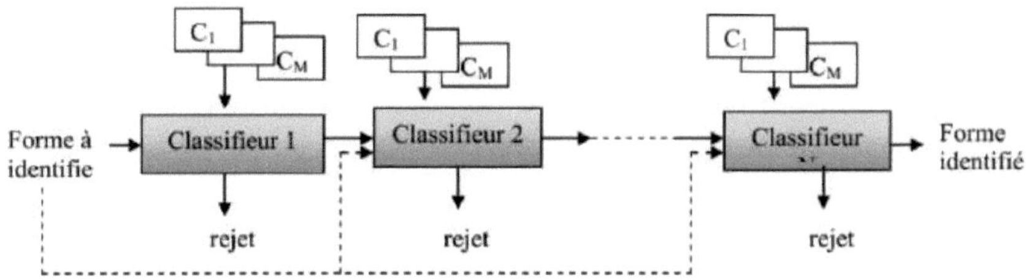



*Figure 3.5: Sequential combination*

This type of combination offers the following advantages:

➢ Progressive decision filtering (ambiguity reduction) ;
➢ The second step (next classifier) is only applied when the first has failed.

On the other hand, the following disadvantages were noted:

➢ It would be necessary to assume a priori knowledge of the behavior of each of the classifiers.
➢ Sensitive to the order in which classifiers are placed

### B. *Parallel combination*

Unlike the sequential approach, the parallel approach first lets the different classifiers operate independently of each other, then merges their respective responses.

This fusion is done either democratically, in the sense that it does not favor one classifier over another, or directionally, in which case the responses of each classifier are assigned a weight according to its performance. The order of execution of the classifiers is not a factor in this approach.

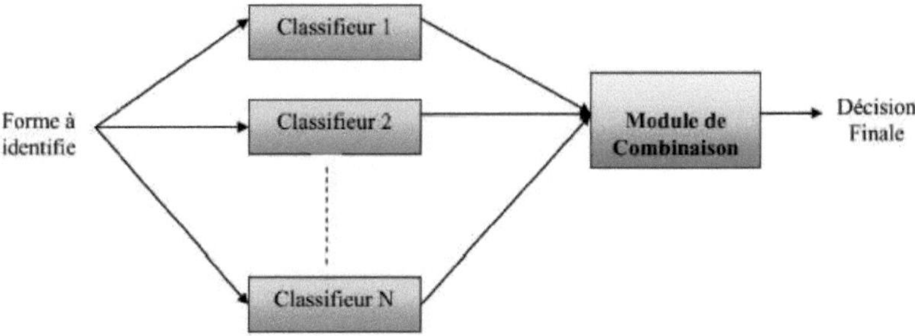



*Figure 3.6: Parallel combination*

This type of combination offers the following advantages:

➢ Very easy to install;
➢ No need to reparameterize other classifiers when modifying the set ;

The following drawback is noted:

➢ On the other hand, it suffers from costly computation time due to the activation of all classifiers.

### C. *Hybrid combination*

This involves combining sequential and parallel approaches, for example, a globally sequential approach that processes rejects from a first method using two other methods operating in parallel.

It combines the advantages of the two previous architectures, enabling :

➢ Reducing the set of possible classes ;
➢ Finding a consensus between classifiers.

This hybridization offers the following advantages:

➢ Take full advantage of each of the classifiers used ;
➢ Numerous combination schemes to make the most of your data.

On the other hand, she suffers from :

➢ Completely dependent on the data to be processed ;
➢ Highly complex to optimize.

It's important that credit card companies are able to recognize fraudulent credit card transactions, so that customers aren't charged for items they haven't purchased.

## 4. SUMMARY

In summary, we have presented set methods for finding a set of hypotheses that are different in their decision making so that they can complement each other, we have also made a study of these methods and then we have presented the three set methods, their principle and algorithm used.

In this chapter, we have presented a formulation of the unbalanced data learning problem with asymmetric classes. This asymmetry generally occurs at two main levels: at class level or at cost level.

We also made a study between different classifiers; this tendency in the scientific community.

We have set out the main elements of the various problems associated with unbalanced databases, as well as a summary of the methods proposed to deal with them. These various methods have been grouped into two main categories: sampling techniques, and asymmetry-sensitive algorithms.

# CHAPTER FOUR :
# EXPERIMENTATION AND INTERPRETATION OF RESULTS

## 1.  INTRODUCTION

In this chapter, we will proceed with the implementation of our model. We'll present the different tools used for implementation, the dataset used, the model architecture and finally, we'll interpret the results.

## 2.  PRESENTATION OF TOOLS USED

To achieve our system, we have made use of a number of software and hardware development tools, which are briefly described below.

### 2.1 The programming environment

As part of our solution, we're going to consider the Python programming language, which is a high-level interpreted, open source, cross-platform, object-oriented language, mainly used for Machine Learning and Data Science. Python has made a major contribution to the rise of artificial intelligence.

Thanks to its many specialized libraries, including Panda, Bokeh, Numpy, Scipy, Scrapy, Matpotlib, Scikit-Learn and TensorFlow, Python can be used in a wide range of situations, such as software development, data analysis, infrastructure management, image processing, scripting and task automation, etc., offering great flexibility in the tasks to be performed and compatibility with all platforms.

The choice of this language is based on its many advantages and features, including: it's free and open source; it's simple and easy to learn; it's readable; it's extensible and can be integrated with other languages; it's object-oriented; it offers a wide range of libraries; it requires less coding; it's portable.

### 2.2 The application development environment

Our model is designed in the PyCharm Professional 2022 environment, a Python integrated development environment developed by the Czech software company JetBrains. It's cross-platform software that runs on Windows, Linux and Mac OS and includes an impressive set of tools, such as intelligent assistance, web development frameworks, scientific tools (like IPython Notebook, Anaconda, NumPy, Matplotlib, etc.), cross-technology development and a huge collection of development tools consisting of a Python tester and debugger, terminal and profiler.), cross-technology development and a huge collection of development tools including a tester and debugger, a terminal and a Python profiler.
Considered the best Python IDE for developers, PyCharm features code analysis and a

graphical debugger. It also offers unit test management, version control integration and support for web development with Django.

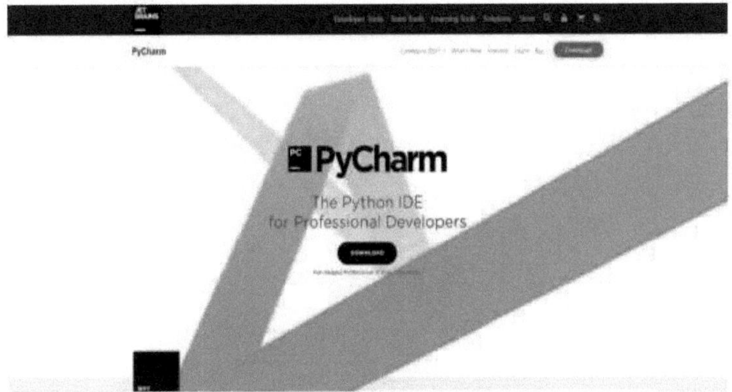

*Figure 4.1: Pycharm IDE*

## DATA PRESENTATION

Our study focuses on the analysis of unbalanced classes for the prediction of
credit card fraud. To this end, we have retrieved the database of the Kaggle website.

The dataset contains credit card transactions made in September 2013 by European cardholders. This dataset shows transactions that occurred over two days, where we have 492 frauds out of 284,807 transactions. The dataset is very unbalanced, with the positive class (frauds) accounting for 0.172% of all transactions.

It contains only numerical input variables which are the result of a PCA transformation. Unfortunately, due to confidentiality issues, we cannot provide the original features and more background information on the data. Features V1, V2,..., V28 are the main components obtained with PCA, the only features not transformed with PCA are 'Time' and 'Amount'.

The 'Time' feature contains the seconds elapsed between each transaction and the first transaction in the dataset. The 'Amount' feature is the transaction amount; this feature can be used for cost-sensitive learning based on the example. The 'Class' feature is the response variable and takes the value 1 in the event of fraud and 0 otherwise.

Given the class imbalance ratio, we recommend measuring precision using the area under the precision recall curve (AUPRC). The precision of the confusion matrix is not significant for unbalanced classification.

|  | Time | V1 | V2 | V3 | V4 | V5 | V6 | V7 | V8 |  |
|---|---|---|---|---|---|---|---|---|---|---|
| 1 | 0 | -1.3598071336738 | -0.07278117330984.. | 2.53634673796914 | 1.37815522427443 | -0.338328769942518 | 0.462387777762292 | 0.239598554061257 | 0.0986979012610507 | 0.36 |
| 2 | 0 | 1.19185711131486 | 0.266150712059063 | 0.16648011335321 | 0.448154078460911 | 0.0600176492822243 | -0.0823608088155687 | -0.0788029833323113 | 0.0851016549148104 | -0.25 |
| 3 | 1 | -1.35835406159823 | -1.34816307473609 | 1.77320934263119 | 0.379779593034328 | -0.503198133318193 | 1.80049938079263 | 0.791460956450422 | 0.247675786588991 | -1.5 |
| 4 | 1 | -0.966271711572087 | -0.185226008082898 | 1.79299333957872 | -0.863291275036453 | -0.0103088796030823 | 1.24720316752486 | 0.23768893977178 | 0.377435874052262 | -1.3 |
| 5 | 2 | -1.15823309349523 | 0.877736754848451 | 1.548717846511 | 0.403033933955121 | -0.407193377311053 | 0.0959214624684256 | 0.592940745385545 | -0.270532677192282 | 0.81 |
| 6 | 2 | -0.425965884412454 | 0.960523044882985 | 1.14110934232219 | -0.168252079768302 | 0.420986880877219 | -0.0297275516639742 | 0.476200948729027 | 0.260314333074874 | -0.5 |
| 7 | 4 | 1.22965763458793 | 0.141003507049326 | 0.0453707735899449 | 1.20261273673594 | 0.191880988597645 | 0.272708122899098 | -0.00515900288250983 | 0.0812129398830894 | 0.46 |
| 8 | 7 | -0.644269442348146 | 1.41796354547385 | 1.0743803763556 | -0.492199018495015 | 0.948934094704157 | 0.428118462833089 | 1.12063135838353 | -3.80786423873589 | 0.61 |
| 9 | 7 | -0.894286080220282 | 0.286157196276544 | -0.113192212729871 | -0.271526130088604 | 2.6695986595986 | 3.72181806112751 | 0.370145127676916 | 0.851084443200905 | -0.39 |
| 10 | 9 | -0.33826175242575 | 1.11959337641566 | 1.04436655157316 | -0.222187276738296 | 0.49936080649727 | -0.24676110061991 | 0.651583206489972 | 0.0695385865186387 | -0.73 |
| 11 | 10 | 1.44904378114715 | -1.17633882535966 | 0.913859832832795 | -1.37566665499943 | -1.97136316545323 | -0.62915213889734 | -1.4232356010359 | 0.0484558879088564 | -1.7 |
| 12 | 10 | 0.38497821518095 | 0.616189459176472 | -0.874299702595852 | -0.0940186259679115 | 2.92458437838817 | 3.31702716826156 | 0.470454671805879 | 0.53824722837695 | -0.55 |
| 13 | 10 | 1.249998742053 | -1.22163680921816 | 0.383938151282291 | -1.23489868766892 | -1.48541947377961 | -0.753230164566149 | -0.689404975426345 | -0.227487227519552 | -2.0 |
| 14 | 11 | 1.0693735878819 | 0.287722129331455 | 0.828612726634281 | 2.71252042961718 | -0.178398016248009 | 0.337543730282968 | -0.0967108617395962 | 0.115981735546597 | -0.22 |
| 15 | 12 | -2.7918547659339 | -0.327770756658058 | 1.64175016056605 | 1.76747274389883 | -0.136588446465306 | 0.80759646826532 | -0.422911389711497 | -1.90710747624096 | 0.75 |
| 16 | 12 | -0.752417042956605 | 0.345485415344747 | 2.05732291278727 | -1.46864329848046 | -1.15839368040082 | -0.0778498291166733 | -0.608581418236123 | 0.00360348436261849 | -0.43 |
| 17 | 12 | 1.16321543528383 | -0.04029621459734.. | 1.2673320885949 | 1.28909146962552 | -0.735997163604068 | 0.288069162976262 | -0.586056786337461 | 0.189379713679593 | 0.78 |
| 18 | 13 | -0.436905071368625 | 0.918966212909322 | 0.92459077438817 | -0.727219053596792 | 0.915678718106307 | -0.127867352079254 | 0.707641607333935 | 0.0879623554672504 | -0.6 |
| 19 | 14 | -5.40125766315825 | -5.45014783428644 | 1.18630463143652 | 1.73623880012895 | 3.04918587764025 | -1.76340557365281 | -1.55973769907953 | 0.160841747266769 | 1.2 |
| 20 | 15 | 1.4929359769862 | -1.02934573189487 | 0.45479473374366 | -1.43802587991702 | -1.55543410136344 | -0.729961147043557 | -1.08066413038614 | -0.0531271179483221 | -1. |
| 21 | 16 | 0.694884775607337 | -1.36181910388009 | 1.02922103956832 | 0.834159299216716 | -1.19120879445965 | 1.30910881872952 | -0.878585911450457 | 0.4452901278385 | -0.44 |
| 22 | 17 | 0.962496069914852 | 0.32846102605212 | -0.17147905415064 | 2.10920486774816 | 1.12956557126894 | 1.6968376856836 | 0.107711607311367 | 0.521502163844302 | -1.1 |
| 23 | 18 | 1.16661638244228 | 0.592120087854101 | -0.0673083143663533 | 2.26156923949128 | 0.428804194630788 | 0.0894735167274599 | 0.241146579907281 | 0.138081705243702 | -0.96 |
| 24 | 18 | 0.247491127783665 | 0.277665627353681 | 1.18547084217971 | -0.0926025498576841 | -1.31439397897870 | -0.158115997622665 | -0.946364950111676 | -1.61793505064675 | 1.5 |
| 25 | 22 | -1.94652513121534 | -0.04498050544181.. | -0.405570068378956 | -1.01305735702394 | 2.94196769950545 | 2.95505339674562 | -0.0630631473635638 | 0.855546309018146 | 0.045 |
| 26 | 22 | -2.0742940722629 | -0.121481799450951 | 1.32202063048967 | 0.410007514171835 | 0.295197545759436 | -0.95953722984438 | 0.543985491287656 | -0.104826728092018 | 0.47 |
| 27 | 23 | 1.17328461817879 | 0.353497878664456 | 0.28390506526532 | 1.1395633178795 | -0.172577181842493 | -0.916053786932115 | 0.36982484539083 | -0.327280242196767 | -0.2 |
| 28 | 23 | 1.32270726911234 | -0.17404083293642 | 0.434555851250987 | 0.576037652384661 | -0.836758645983797 | -0.831083411483829 | -0.264904960791055 | -0.220981942667704 | -1.0 |
| 29 | 23 | -0.414288810090829 | 0.905437322625407 | 1.72745294417921 | 1.47347126657189 | 0.00744274117322988 | -0.200338677416199 | 0.740228319420026 | -0.029247400012072 | -0.55 |
| 30 | 23 | 1.05938711501788 | -0.175319186719244 | 1.26612964251002 | 1.18610995469348 | -0.786001752758539 | 0.578435276462307 | -0.767084276374229 | 0.401046149117525 | 0.65 |
| 31 | 24 | 1.23742903021294 | 0.0610425841868962 | 0.380525879794222 | 0.761564111432371 | -0.359770710369787 | -0.494084149915291 | 0.00649421810779282 | -0.133862379689891 | 0.43 |
| 32 | 25 | 1.11400859541157 | 0.0855460896870318 | 0.493702487395368 | 1.33575998514475 | -0.308188550958467 | -0.0107537834263628 | -0.11876001589605 | 0.188616695943139 | 0.2 |
| 33 | 26 | -0.529912284186556 | 0.873891581460326 | 1.34724732930113 | 0.145456676582257 | 0.414209858362661 | 0.10022309405219 | 0.711206082959649 | 0.1760659570625 | -0.28 |

Large File Editor   Data

*Figure 4.2: Extract of imported data*

# 3.    MODEL IMPLEMENTATION

The development of our model is divided into the following main phases: pre-processing, learning and testing. As shown in the diagram below

We will predict credit card fraud based on the various dataset values as defined above.

## 3.1.    Importing libraries

➢    **Pandas**: Pandas is a library written for the Python programming language, enabling data manipulation and analysis. In particular, it provides data structures and operations for manipulating numerical arrays and time series.
!pip install pandas

➢    **Numpy**: Numpy is a library for the Python programming language, designed to manipulate matrices or multidimensional arrays, as well as mathematical functions operating on these arrays.
More specifically, this free, open source software library provides a wide range of functions for creating an array directly from a file or saving an array to a file, and for manipulating vectors, matrices and polynomials.

Using Numpy in python offers features comparable to those of Matlab, as they are both

interpreted. Both allow the user to write fast programs by performing operations on arrays or matrices instead of scalars. Matlab has a large number of additional toolboxes, such as simulink. Numpy, on the other hand, is intrinsically integrated with python, a more recent and complete programming language, and complementary python libraries are available.
!pip install numpy

➢ **Matplotlib**: Matplotlib is a Python programming language library for plotting and visualizing data in graphical form. It can be combined with the NumPy and SciPy scientific computing libraries.
!pip install matplotlib

➢ **Seaborn**: Seaborn is a Python data visualization library based on matplotlib . It provides a high-level interface for drawing attractive and informative statistical graphs.
!pip install seaborn

➢ **Scikit-learn**: Scikit-learn is a free Python library for machine learning. It has been developed by numerous contributors, notably in the academic world by French higher education and research institutes such as Inria.
Its framework includes a number of libraries of algorithms that can be implemented on a turnkey basis. These libraries are particularly useful for data scientists. They include functions for estimating random forests, logistic regressions, classification algorithms and support vector machines. It is designed to harmonize with other free Python libraries, notably NumPy and SciPy.
!pip install scikit-learn

➢ **Imblearn**: Imbalanced-learn (imported as imblearn) is an MIT-licensed open source library that builds on scikit-learn (imported as sklearn) and provides tools for managing classification with unbalanced classes.
!pip install imblearn

➢ ***Source code***

```
import pandas as pd import numpy as np
from matplotlib import pyplot as plt import seaborn as sns
from sklearn import preprocessing
from sklearn.metrics import classification_report, confusion_matrix, roc curve,
roc_auc_score,auc, accuracy_score
from sklearn.linear_model import LogisticRegression

from sklearn.model_selection import train_test_split from IPython.core.display import
HTML
```

## 3.2.    Data standardization

We create the function that allows us to standardize the quantitative data (cont_feat is a list of columns corresponding to quantitative characteristics) to bring the variables to the level to facilitate the equitable treatment of all columns :

```
def scale_feat(df,cont_feat): df1=df
scaler = preprocessing.RobustScaler() df1[cont_feat] = scaler.fit_transform(df1[cont_feat])
return df1
```

## 3.3.        Tracing learning curves

The function for plotting learning curves on the learning set and the validation set to enable us to study the trends in the curves:

```
def plot_roc_curve(est,X_test,y_test): probas = est.predict_proba(X_test)
false_positive_rate, true_positive_rate, thresholds = roc_curve(y_test,probas[:, 1]) roc_auc =
auc(false_positive_rate, true_positive_rate)
plt.figure(figsize=(8,8))
plt.title('Receiver Operating Characteristic')
plt.plot(false_positive_rate, true_positive_rate, 'b', label='AUC = %0.2f'% roc_auc)
plt.legend(loc='lower right')
plt.plot([0,1],[0,1],'r--')
plt.plot([0,0,1],[0,1,1],'g:')
plt.xlim([-0.05,1.2])
plt.ylim([-0.05,1.2]) plt.ylabel('True positive rate') plt.xlabel('False positive rate') plt.show
```

## 3.4.        Dataset processing

We start by importing the dataset and displaying its first five rows to represent all the columns:

```
df = pd.read_csv("creditcard.csv") df.head().T
```

|  | 0 | 1 | 2 | 3 | 4 |
|---|---|---|---|---|---|
| Time | 0.000000 | 0.000000 | 1.000000 | 1.000000 | 2.000000 |
| V1 | -1.359807 | 1.191857 | -1.358354 | -0.966272 | -1.158233 |
| V2 | -0.072781 | 0.266151 | -1.340163 | -0.185226 | 0.877737 |
| V3 | 2.536347 | 0.166480 | 1.773209 | 1.792993 | 1.548718 |
| V4 | 1.378155 | 0.448154 | 0.379780 | -0.863291 | 0.403034 |
| V5 | -0.338321 | 0.060018 | -0.503198 | -0.010309 | -0.407193 |
| V6 | 0.462388 | -0.082361 | 1.800499 | 1.247203 | 0.095921 |
| V7 | 0.239599 | -0.078803 | 0.791461 | 0.237609 | 0.592941 |
| V8 | 0.098698 | 0.085102 | 0.247676 | 0.377436 | -0.270533 |
| V9 | 0.363787 | -0.255425 | -1.514654 | -1.387024 | 0.817739 |
| V10 | 0.090794 | -0.166974 | 0.207643 | -0.054952 | 0.753074 |
| V11 | -0.551600 | 1.612727 | 0.624501 | -0.226487 | -0.822843 |
| V12 | -0.617801 | 1.065235 | 0.066084 | 0.178228 | 0.538196 |
| V13 | -0.991390 | 0.489095 | 0.717293 | 0.507757 | 1.345852 |
| V14 | -0.311169 | -0.143772 | -0.165946 | -0.287924 | -1.119670 |
| V15 | 1.468177 | 0.635558 | 2.345865 | -0.631418 | 0.175121 |
| V16 | -0.470401 | 0.463917 | -2.890083 | -1.059647 | -0.451449 |
| V17 | 0.207971 | -0.114805 | 1.109969 | -0.684093 | -0.237033 |
| V18 | 0.025791 | -0.183361 | -0.121359 | 1.965775 | -0.038195 |
| V19 | 0.403993 | -0.145783 | -2.261857 | -1.232622 | 0.803487 |
| V20 | 0.251412 | -0.069083 | 0.524980 | -0.208038 | 0.408542 |
| V21 | -0.018307 | -0.225775 | 0.247998 | -0.108300 | -0.009431 |
| V22 | 0.277838 | -0.638672 | 0.771679 | 0.005274 | 0.798278 |
| V23 | -0.110474 | 0.101288 | 0.909412 | -0.190321 | -0.137458 |
| V24 | 0.066928 | -0.339846 | -0.689281 | -1.175575 | 0.141267 |
| V25 | 0.128539 | 0.167170 | -0.327642 | 0.647376 | -0.206010 |
| V26 | -0.189115 | 0.125895 | -0.139097 | -0.221929 | 0.502292 |
| V27 | 0.133558 | -0.008983 | -0.055353 | 0.062723 | 0.219422 |
| V28 | -0.021053 | 0.014724 | -0.059752 | 0.061458 | 0.215153 |
| Amount | 149.620000 | 2.690000 | 378.660000 | 123.500000 | 69.990000 |
| Class | 0.000000 | 0.000000 | 0.000000 | 0.000000 | 0.000000 |

*Figure 4.3: Extract from the database*

We display the statistical details of the imported database instances to give us a global and detailed view of the dataset data, and also to see if data is missing on certain lines: df.describe().T

|        | count    | mean          | std         | min          | 25%          | 50%          | 75%          | max          |
| --- | --- | --- | --- | --- | --- | --- | --- | --- |
| Time   | 284807.0 | 9.481386e+04  | 47488.145955 | 0.000000    | 54201.500000 | 84692.000000 | 139320.500000 | 172792.000000 |
| V1     | 284807.0 | 1.168375e-15  | 1.958696    | -56.407510  | -0.920373   | 0.018109    | 1.315642    | 2.454930    |
| V2     | 284807.0 | 3.416908e-16  | 1.651309    | -72.715728  | -0.598550   | 0.065486    | 0.803724    | 22.057729   |
| V3     | 284807.0 | -1.379537e-15 | 1.516255    | -48.325589  | -0.890365   | 0.179846    | 1.027196    | 9.382558    |
| V4     | 284807.0 | 2.074095e-15  | 1.415869    | -5.683171   | -0.848640   | -0.019847   | 0.743341    | 16.875344   |
| V5     | 284807.0 | 9.604066e-16  | 1.380247    | -113.743307 | -0.691597   | -0.054336   | 0.611926    | 34.801666   |
| V6     | 284807.0 | 1.487313e-15  | 1.332271    | -26.160506  | -0.768296   | -0.274187   | 0.398565    | 73.301626   |
| V7     | 284807.0 | -5.556467e-16 | 1.237094    | -43.557242  | -0.554076   | 0.040103    | 0.570436    | 120.589494  |
| V8     | 284807.0 | 1.213481e-16  | 1.194353    | -73.216718  | -0.208630   | 0.022358    | 0.327346    | 20.007208   |
| V9     | 284807.0 | -2.406331e-15 | 1.098632    | -13.434066  | -0.643098   | -0.051429   | 0.597139    | 15.594995   |
| V10    | 284807.0 | 2.239053e-15  | 1.088850    | -24.588262  | -0.535426   | -0.092917   | 0.453923    | 23.745136   |
| V11    | 284807.0 | 1.673327e-15  | 1.020713    | -4.797473   | -0.762494   | -0.032757   | 0.739593    | 12.018913   |
| V12    | 284807.0 | -1.247012e-15 | 0.999201    | -18.683715  | -0.405571   | 0.140033    | 0.618238    | 7.848392    |
| V13    | 284807.0 | 8.190001e-16  | 0.995274    | -5.791881   | -0.648539   | -0.013568   | 0.662505    | 7.126883    |
| V14    | 284807.0 | 1.207294e-15  | 0.958596    | -19.214325  | -0.425574   | 0.050601    | 0.493150    | 10.526766   |
| V15    | 284807.0 | 4.887456e-15  | 0.915316    | -4.498945   | -0.582884   | 0.048072    | 0.648821    | 8.877742    |
| V16    | 284807.0 | 1.437716e-15  | 0.876253    | -14.129855  | -0.468037   | 0.066413    | 0.523296    | 17.315112   |
| V17    | 284807.0 | -3.772171e-16 | 0.849337    | -25.162799  | -0.483748   | -0.065676   | 0.399675    | 9.253526    |
| V18    | 284807.0 | 9.564149e-16  | 0.838176    | -9.498746   | -0.498850   | -0.003636   | 0.500807    | 5.041069    |
| V19    | 284807.0 | 1.039917e-15  | 0.814041    | -7.213527   | -0.456299   | 0.003735    | 0.458949    | 5.591971    |
| V20    | 284807.0 | 6.406204e-16  | 0.770925    | -54.497720  | -0.211721   | -0.062481   | 0.133041    | 39.420904   |
| V21    | 284807.0 | 1.654067e-16  | 0.734524    | -34.830382  | -0.228395   | -0.029450   | 0.186377    | 27.202839   |
| V22    | 284807.0 | -3.568593e-16 | 0.725702    | -10.933144  | -0.542350   | 0.006782    | 0.528554    | 10.503090   |
| V23    | 284807.0 | 2.578648e-16  | 0.624460    | -44.807735  | -0.161846   | -0.011193   | 0.147642    | 22.528412   |
| V24    | 284807.0 | 4.473266e-15  | 0.605647    | -2.836627   | -0.354586   | 0.040976    | 0.439527    | 4.584549    |
| V25    | 284807.0 | 5.340915e-16  | 0.521278    | -10.295397  | -0.317145   | 0.016594    | 0.350716    | 7.519589    |
| V26    | 284807.0 | 1.683437e-15  | 0.482227    | -2.604551   | -0.326984   | -0.052139   | 0.240952    | 3.517346    |
| V27    | 284807.0 | -3.660091e-16 | 0.403632    | -22.565679  | -0.070840   | 0.001342    | 0.091045    | 31.612198   |
| V28    | 284807.0 | -1.227390e-16 | 0.330083    | -15.430084  | -0.052960   | 0.011244    | 0.078280    | 33.847808   |
| Amount | 284807.0 | 8.834962e+01  | 250.120109  | 0.000000    | 5.600000    | 22.000000   | 77.165000   | 25691.160000 |
| Class  | 284807.0 | 1.727486e-03  | 0.041527    | 0.000000    | 0.000000    | 0.000000    | 0.000000    | 1.000000    |

*Figure 4.4: Distribution of instances in the training set*

We check the dataset for imbalance:

```
In 15   1   df.Class.value_counts()

Out 15  ∨     0     284315
              1        492
        Name: Class, dtype: int64
```

*Figure 4.5: Checking dataset imbalance*

We note that the data in our dataset is very unbalanced, with only 492 fraudulent transactions compared with 284315 non-fraudulent transactions, representing 99.827% of non-fraudulent transactions and 0.172% of fraudulent transactions.

We check for null values or missing values in
the dataset :

```
In 16   1   df.isnull().values.sum()
```

```
Out 16      0
```



We call the standardization function created above :

cont_feat = list(set(df.columns)-{'Class'}) df=scale_feat(df,cont_feat) df[cont_feat].describe().T

| | count | mean | std | min | 25% | 50% | 75% | max |
|---|---|---|---|---|---|---|---|---|
| V2 | 284807.0 | -0.046700 | 1.177594 | -51.902285 | -0.473542 | 0.0 | 0.526458 | 15.683274 |
| V16 | 284807.0 | -0.066994 | 0.883914 | -14.320381 | -0.539123 | 0.0 | 0.460877 | 17.399498 |
| V9 | 284807.0 | 0.041467 | 0.885825 | -10.790391 | -0.477061 | 0.0 | 0.522939 | 12.615676 |
| V6 | 284807.0 | 0.234978 | 1.141757 | -22.184587 | -0.423451 | 0.0 | 0.576549 | 63.054506 |
| V13 | 284807.0 | 0.010349 | 0.759146 | -4.407413 | -0.484325 | 0.0 | 0.515675 | 5.446384 |
| V28 | 284807.0 | -0.085674 | 2.515117 | -117.657402 | -0.489209 | 0.0 | 0.510791 | 257.822531 |
| V8 | 284807.0 | -0.041715 | 2.228372 | -136.646287 | -0.430967 | 0.0 | 0.569033 | 37.286865 |
| Time | 284807.0 | 0.118914 | 0.557903 | -0.994983 | -0.358210 | 0.0 | 0.641790 | 1.035022 |
| V4 | 284807.0 | 0.012467 | 0.889375 | -3.557406 | -0.520605 | 0.0 | 0.479395 | 10.612681 |
| V27 | 284807.0 | -0.008291 | 2.493334 | -139.401862 | -0.445883 | 0.0 | 0.554117 | 195.267780 |
| V23 | 284807.0 | 0.036166 | 2.017718 | -144.743845 | -0.486782 | 0.0 | 0.513218 | 72.828591 |
| V26 | 284807.0 | 0.091805 | 0.849087 | -4.494188 | -0.483936 | 0.0 | 0.516064 | 6.285011 |
| V12 | 284807.0 | -0.136776 | 0.975964 | -18.385986 | -0.532916 | 0.0 | 0.467084 | 7.529095 |
| V24 | 284807.0 | -0.051600 | 0.762671 | -3.623671 | -0.498118 | 0.0 | 0.501882 | 5.721572 |
| V21 | 284807.0 | 0.071003 | 1.770910 | -83.903734 | -0.479648 | 0.0 | 0.520352 | 65.656022 |
| V11 | 284807.0 | 0.021808 | 0.679530 | -3.172063 | -0.485815 | 0.0 | 0.514185 | 8.023281 |
| V17 | 284807.0 | 0.074342 | 0.961416 | -28.408945 | -0.473241 | 0.0 | 0.526759 | 10.548966 |
| Amount | 284807.0 | 0.927124 | 3.495006 | -0.307413 | -0.229162 | 0.0 | 0.770838 | 358.683155 |
| V5 | 284807.0 | 0.041684 | 1.058858 | -87.216663 | -0.488876 | 0.0 | 0.511124 | 26.739834 |
| V10 | 284807.0 | 0.093918 | 1.100572 | -24.759049 | -0.447272 | 0.0 | 0.552728 | 24.094682 |
| V1 | 284807.0 | -0.008099 | 0.875976 | -25.234901 | -0.419712 | 0.0 | 0.580288 | 1.089805 |
| V14 | 284807.0 | -0.055078 | 1.043399 | -20.969224 | -0.518301 | 0.0 | 0.481699 | 11.402953 |
| V7 | 284807.0 | -0.035663 | 1.100116 | -38.770014 | -0.528388 | 0.0 | 0.471612 | 107.201520 |
| V20 | 284807.0 | 0.181230 | 2.236107 | -157.892131 | -0.432879 | 0.0 | 0.567121 | 114.523532 |
| V22 | 284807.0 | -0.006333 | 0.677653 | -10.215599 | -0.512775 | 0.0 | 0.487225 | 9.801353 |
| V3 | 284807.0 | -0.093789 | 0.790721 | -25.295389 | -0.558111 | 0.0 | 0.441889 | 4.799177 |
| V15 | 284807.0 | -0.039028 | 0.743129 | -3.691644 | -0.512262 | 0.0 | 0.487738 | 7.168656 |
| V25 | 284807.0 | -0.024846 | 0.780519 | -15.440333 | -0.499713 | 0.0 | 0.500287 | 11.234373 |
| V19 | 284807.0 | -0.004081 | 0.889420 | -7.885579 | -0.502633 | 0.0 | 0.497367 | 6.105706 |
| V18 | 284807.0 | 0.003638 | 0.838464 | -9.498372 | -0.495384 | 0.0 | 0.504616 | 5.046439 |



We display the distributions of continuous values:
for col in cont_feat : plt.figure(figsize=[10,5]) plt.title(col) sns.kdeplot(df[col])

*Figure 4.8: Extract from a distribution of continuous values*

It's a bit difficult to study the figures since we don't know what they refer to.

## 3.5.        Random Forest

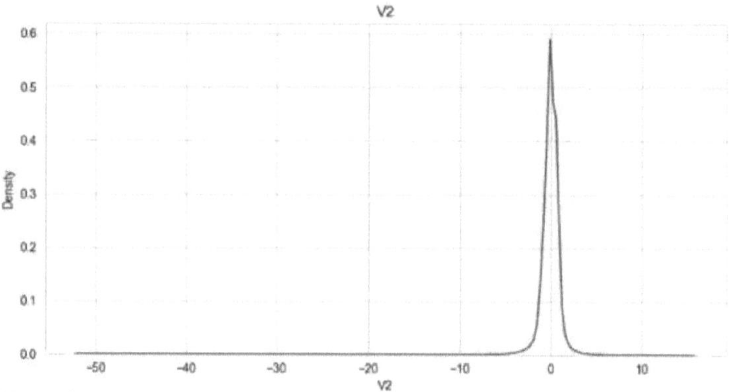



One of the great challenges of machine learning in recent years has been the explicability or interpretability of models.

Its efficiency is quite good, and we have techniques for interpreting the results. For example, we can determine which features (columns) were decisive in obtaining a prediction. Random forest offers greater transparency on the use made of training data.

We build the training and test sets, i.e. we divide our dataset by creating two classes of data X and Y :

X = df.drop(['Class'], axis=1) y = df.Class
X_train, X_test, y_train, y_test = train_test_split(X, y, test_size=0.2, random_state=1) : We draw only 20% of the data for the test and control the randomness so that we have the same data each time we train the data.

We test random forests:

from sklearn import ensemble
rf = ensemble.RandomForestClassifier() rf.fit(X_train, y_train)
y_rf = rf.predict(X_test) print(classification_report(y_test, y_rf))
pd.crosstab(y_test, y_rf, rownames=['Reel'], colnames=['Prediction'], margins=True)

50

```
In 24  1  print(classification_report(y_test, y_rf))

              precision    recall  f1-score   support

           0       1.00      1.00      1.00     56875
           1       0.93      0.76      0.84        87

    accuracy                           1.00     56962
   macro avg       0.96      0.88      0.92     56962
weighted avg       1.00      1.00      1.00     56962


In 25  1  pd.crosstab(y_test, y_rf, rownames=['Reel'], colnames=['Prediction'], margins=True)

Out 25    Prediction        0        1      All
          Reel

                   0    56870        5    56875
                   1       21       66       87
                 All    56891       71    56962
```

*Figure 4.9: Result of random forest test*

The model has an accuracy of 1, which is a very good result. For the class of non-fraudulent transactions, we have 56875 good transactions and we manage to classify the data 100% accurately, and we have 87 fraudulent transactions that we manage to classify 93% accurately.

As for the confusion matrix, since we're using binary classification, our matrix has 4 cells, i.e. two rows and two columns; on the rows where we have the real results and on the columns where we have the predicted results, we say that for a total of 56875 non-fraudulent transactions, after processing, the model found that 56870 or 99,991% were non-fraudulent transactions, i.e. true positives, and only 5 transactions, i.e. 0.008%, were fraudulent transactions, i.e. false positives. Out of a total of 87 fraudulent transactions, the model correctly classified 66, i.e. 75.862%, as true negatives, and 21 incorrectly classified transactions, i.e. 24.137%, as false negatives.

## 3.6.        Subsampling

We have found that there are far fewer fraudulent transactions than non-fraudulent ones.
We're going to keep as many non-fraudulent transactions as fraudulent ones in the training set (X_train), randomly selecting the ones we're going to keep. We say we're "sub-sampling the majority class".

from imblearn.under_sampling import RandomUnderSampler rus = RandomUnderSampler()
X_train, y_train = rus.fit_resample(X_train, y_train)

We check that we have balanced the training set: y_train.value_counts()

```
In 28   1 │ y_train.value_counts()
```

```
Out 28  ∨   0    405
            1    405
          Name: Class, dtype: int64
```
*Figure 4.10: Balancing the training set*

We apply random forests to the new training set:

rf = ensemble.RandomForestClassifier() rf.fit(X_train, y_train)
y_rf = rf.predict(X_test) print(classification_report(y_test, y_rf))
pd.crosstab(y_test, y_rf, rownames=['Reel'], colnames=['Prediction'], margins=True)

```
In 29   1 │ rf = ensemble.RandomForestClassifier()
        2 │ rf.fit(X_train, y_train)
        3 │ y_rf = rf.predict(X_test)
        4 │
        5 │ print(classification_report(y_test, y_rf))
        6 │
        7 │ pd.crosstab(y_test, y_rf, rownames=['Reel'], colnames=['Prediction'], margins=True)
```

```
              precision   recall  f1-score   support

           0       1.00     0.97      0.99     56875
           1       0.05     0.90      0.10        87

    accuracy                          0.97     56962
   macro avg       0.53     0.94      0.54     56962
weighted avg       1.00     0.97      0.99     56962
```

```
Out 29  ∨   Prediction     0        1       All
            Reel

                     0   55418     1457     56875
                     1       9       78        87
                   All   55427     1535     56962
```

*Figure 4.11: Subsampling result*

True positives were 55418 out of 56875 (99.128%), false positives were 1457 out of 56875 (2.561%), true negatives were 78 out of 87 (89.655%) and false negatives were 9 out of 87 (10.344%).

We have less training data, but the results are slightly better for fraud detection (78 out of 87).

## 3.7.          Oversampling

We're going to rebalance the dataset by oversampling the minority class - we've found that there are far more non-fraudulent transactions than fraudulent ones.

We will duplicate as many fraudulent transactions as non-fraudulent ones, thus creating "false" (but "plausible") data for learning purposes:

```python
from imblearn.over_sampling import SMOTE smote = SMOTE()
X_train, y_train = smote.fit_resample(X_train, y_train) y_train.value_counts()
```

We have balanced the training set (by "adding" data); We test the random forests with the oversampled data:

```python
from sklearn import ensemble
rf = ensemble.RandomForestClassifier() rf.fit(X_train, y_train)
y_rf = rf.predict(X_test)

print(classification_report(y_test, y_rf))
pd.crosstab(y_test, y_rf, rownames=['Reel'], colnames=['Prediction'], margins=True)
```

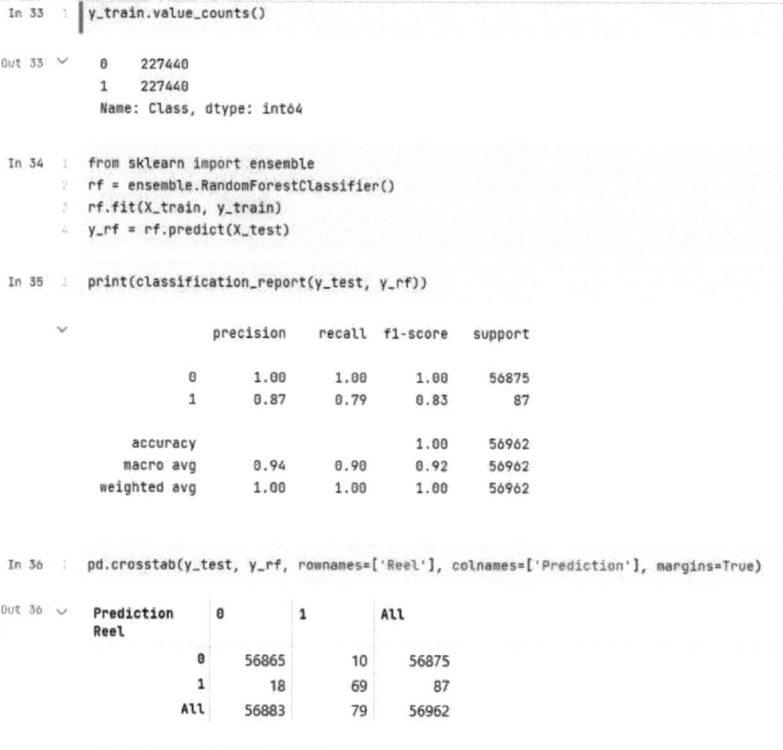



*Figure 4.12: Oversampling result*

The true positive is 56865 out of 56875 or 99.982%, the false positive is 10 out of 56875 or 0.017%, the true negative is 69 out of 87 or 79.310% and the false negative is 18 out of 87 or 20.689%.

The results are good, but not as good as those of the two previous models.

## 4.    RESULTS INTERPRETATION

In the light of the above experiments, we have concluded that our problem can be solved using several models, all of which have equivalent accuracies, such as Random Forest.

For the random forest, we found that for a total of 56875 non-fraudulent transactions, after processing, the model found that 56870 or 99.991% were non-fraudulent transactions, i.e. true positives, and only 5 transactions or 0.008% were fraudulent transactions, i.e. false positives, and out of a total of 87 fraudulent transactions, the model correctly classified 66 or 75.862% as true negatives and 21 or 24.137% as false negatives.

For the sub-sampling, the true positive is 55418 out of 56875 or 99.128%, the false positive is 1457 out of 56875 or 2.561%, the true negative is 78 out of 87 or 89.655% and the false negative is 9 out of 87 or 10.344%.

For oversampling, the true positive is 56865 out of 56875 or 99.982%, the false positive is 10 out of 56875 or 0.017%, the true negative is 69 out of 87 or 79.310% and the false negative is 18 out of 87 or 20.689%.

After our study, we found that the class of non-fraudulent transactions is the best classified using random forest, as the model manages to give 100% accuracy in classifying the data, and the same goes for fraudulent transactions, with a classification accuracy of 93%, compared with other methods which give us lower accuracies.

We note that, despite the imbalance in our dataset, Random Forest is best suited to our data because the accuracies it gives are better than those of the other two methods, and the results are quite good. On the other hand, the oversampling and undersampling methods do not improve the performance of the algorithms.

## 5.    SUMMARY

This chapter has illustrated that the design of a basic fraud detection system can be achieved using simple pre-processing strategies and standard machine learning classifiers. In particular, we have succeeded in achieving fraud detection performance well above that of a random classifier.

However, the chapter has only scratched the surface of how to approach a fraud detection problem. As we know, many more advanced techniques can be used to improve performance. Performance can be approached in terms of fraud detection accuracy, but also in terms of computational requirements (memory/runtime).

The latter is important in practice during training, as fraud detection systems need to process large amounts of data (much higher than those used in this basic example) and also during inference for real-time or near-real-time processing. Trade-offs between accuracy and computational requirements generally need to be carefully considered.

# GENERAL CONCLUSION

The aim of our study was to build a prediction model using assembly methods to improve the performance of an individual classifier for handling unbalanced datasets.

Detecting fraudulent patterns in payment card transactions is notoriously difficult. With the ever-increasing amount of data generated by payment card transactions, it has become impossible for a human analyst to detect fraudulent patterns in transaction datasets, often characterized by a large number of samples, many dimensions and online updates. As a result, the design of payment card fraud detection techniques has increasingly focused over the last decade on approaches based on machine learning techniques, which automate the process of identifying fraudulent patterns from large volumes of data.

To achieve our objective, we used the random forest, a method that combines several decision trees to arrive at an optimal decision. We also used the subsampling and oversampling methods to achieve the same results, and finally drew a conclusion on the three methods used, which we implemented using the phyton programming language.

After our analysis, we noted and concluded that the random forest method is the most suitable for our study, as the model is able to give a good accuracy of up to 100% in classifying data for non-fraudulent transactions and the same for fraudulent transactions, with a classification accuracy of 93% compared with other methods which give us lower accuracies.

Looking ahead, in future work we propose to test the effectiveness of another solution, such as the use of heterogeneous combination, in order to benefit from the advantages of each individual classifier.

In conclusion, we hope that this modest work has made a contribution, however small, to this vast field of research, which is at once interesting, challenging and topical, without, however, claiming to be perfect.

# BIBLIOGRAPHY


## I.  WORKS

1.      A. CONUEJOLS, L. MICLET and Y. KODRATOFF, Apprentissage artificiel :
Concepts et algorithmes, ed. Eyrolles 2003

2.      L. BREIMAN, Arcing classifiers, The Annals of Statistics, vol. 26, no. 3, 1998.

3.      L. BREIMAN, Randon Forest Machine Learning. California, 2001.

4.      L BREIMAN, J.H. FRIEDMAN, R.A. OLSHEN and C.J. STONE. Classification And
Regression Trees. New York, 1984.

5.      Guillaume Saint-Cirgue, Learn machine learning in a week, 2019 Edition. P.36, 37

6.      HARRINGTON Peter, Machine Learning in Action, MANNING 2012

7.      M. LICHMAN. UCI machine learning repository, 2013.

8.      V NITESH, W. Bowyer, O. Lawrence HALL, and W. Philip KEGELMEYER. Smote:
Synthetic minority over-sampling technique Journal of Artificial Intelligence and Research,
2002.

9.      Nickerson A., N. Japkowiez and E. Milios Using unsupervised learning to guide
resampling in imbalanced data set In Proceedings of the Eighth International Workshop on
Artificial Intelligence and Statistics, 2001.

10.     Chao Chen, Andy Liaw and Breiman, L., Using Random Forest to Learn Imbalanced
Data. Machine Learning, 2001.


## II.     THESES AND ARTICLES

8.      Thesis by LABARRE Mélanie, comparison of ensemblist methods, Université de
Montréal, June 2003

9.      Thesis by HAMDI Fatama, Learning in unbalanced distributions, Université Paris 13,
December 2012

10.     Rahman, A. and Fairhurst, M. Multiple classifier decision combination strategies for
character recognition: a review. Journal Document Analysis and Recognition JDAR, 2003

11.     Laurent Rouvière, Introduction to aggregation methods: boosting, bagging and random
forests. Illustrations with R. University of Rennes 2

12.     Henri-Maxime Suchier. New Contributions of Boosting in Machine Learning. PhD
thesis, Université Jean Monnet de Saint-Etienne, 2006.

13.     Stanislas Lauly, Exploring autoencoder-based neural networks in textual data
modeling, Thesis, Sherbrooke University, Quebec, Canada, August 6, 2016, P.5, 7, 8, 14 , 16,
17, 18


## III.    COURSE NOTES

14.     Fabien Teytaud, Artificial learning course, Université du Littoral Côte d'Opale 30
october 2018 P.3

15.     Kafunda Katalay P, datawarehouse, note de cours Université de Kinshasa 2016

16.     Professor Doctor Kafunda Katalay, Artificial intelligence course notes

second degree in computer engineering, University of Mbuji-Mayi, 2021.

17.	Mokhtar Taffar Enseignant-Chercheur-Support de Cours Initiation à l'apprentissage automatic Univ.-Jijel

18.	PREUX Ph., Fouille de données, Notes de cours Université de Lille 3, August 31, 2009

## IV.	MEMORY

19.	DERKOUI A. and DERKOUI S. Etude comparative des méthodes ensemblistes de classification des données médicales, Université Abou Bakr Belkaïd de Tlemcen, September 2017.

20.	KANKOLONGO A. Development of an intrusion detection system model, University of Mbujimayi, 2018

21.	NGELEKA S., the reduction of false rejections and false acceptances of banking information, University of Mbujimayi ,2017-2018

22.	NKASHAMA KANDA D., Supervised Learning based on Vast Separators

23.	Margin for intrusion detection Application to the problem of unbalanced classes, University of Kinshasa, 2015-2016

24.	KELLY K., Artificial learning based on classifier combination by AdaBoost for performance improvement of weak learning algorithms, University of Kinshasa 2012.

# WEBOGRAPHY


25.	https://blog.octo.com/les-methodes-ensemblistes-pour-algorithmes-de-machine-earning

le 14-10-2022 ; 19:39

26.	https://www.quantmetry.com/single-post/2017/02/02/Classification-upervis%C3%A9e-

et-Asym%C3%A9trie on 14-10-2022; 22:17

27.	http://www.u-picardie.fr/~furst/apprentissage.php on 07/11/2022; 21:27

28.	http://www.wikipedia.com/Apprentissage automatic.htm on 01-05-2022 ; 18:26

29.	https://seaborn.pydata.org/ on 11-25-2022; 23:39

30.	https://www.kaggle.com/datasets/mlg-ulb/creditcardfraud on 17-10-2022; 07:23

31.	https://imbalanced-learn.org/stable/ on 26-11-2022; 01:03

Printed by Books on Demand GmbH, Norderstedt / Germany